W9-AOZ-074

# Inclusive Education
# in the Middle East

# Routledge Research in Education

*For a full list of titles in this series, please visit www.routledge.com*

# Inclusive Education in the Middle East

## Eman Gaad

Routledge
Taylor & Francis Group
New York   London

First published 2011
by Routledge
270 Madison Avenue, New York, NY 10016

Simultaneously published in the UK
by Routledge
2 Park Square, Milton Park, Abingdon, Oxon OX14 4RN

*Routledge is an imprint of the Taylor & Francis Group, an informa business*

© 2011 Taylor & Francis

The right of Eman Gaad to be identified as author of this work has been asserted by her in accordance with sections 77 and 78 of the Copyright, Designs and Patents Act 1988.

Typeset in Sabon by IBT Global.
Printed and bound in the United States of America on acid-free paper by IBT Global.

*Library of Congress Cataloging-in-Publication Data*
Gaad, Eman.
  Inclusive education in the Middle East / By Eman Gaad.
    p. cm. — (Routledge research in education ; v.41)
  Includes bibliographical references and index.
  1. Inclusive education—Middle East.  2. Education and state—Middle
East.  I. Title.
  LC1203.M65G33 2010
  371.9'0460956—dc22
                                            2010007401

ISBN13: 978-0-415-99881-9 (hbk)
ISBN13: 978-0-203-84521-9 (ebk)

*To my late mother Bodoor, as you liked to be called. Not a day goes by without thinking of something I learned from you. Your "inclusive" values infected me for life and made me who I am today. . . . I will be grateful until the day we meet again . . . may you rest in peace.*

To all those who are marginalized and excluded because they differ in race, gender, religion, origin, features, or abilities . . . hang in there . . . the norm is inclusion . . . if we are not there yet, it does not mean that we will be here forever. Meanwhile, let us keep paving the way for next generations. Change does not occur coincidentally. The world can change only if we want to change it.

# Contents

# Figures and Tables

# Acknowledgments

I wish to thank those who helped me through this exciting and rather enlightening journey. My family was simply the main source of inspiration when I was drowning in data from nine different countries. My husband Esam, thank you for believing in me and for staying up with me when I was falling asleep on the computer screen buried under papers. My son Shaddy and my daughter Maha, thanks for your understanding when I needed it most.

During the research period, I was fortunate to know many supporters and friends on my visits to the different countries. Friends like Nagwa Madani from Kuwait went beyond the line of friendship and/or professional duties to supply me with data.

I was inspired by a few people with special needs from around the region. Deena Galal from Egypt, a Special Olympic Champion with a heart of gold, and Ola Abu Alghaib from Palestine who helped women with disability to find their independence in a war zone through Starts of Hope. I wish to thank a few organizations that fight for the inclusion of people with special needs in and outside of education such as UAE Down Syndrome Association and Indemaj UAE.

Technical support is much appreciated. I am grateful to Rose Oconnor for proof reading and to Roya Thabet for translating some data. Max Novick was a very helpful editor indeed with his prompt replies and supportive remarks as well as Michael Watters from Integrated Book Technology, Inc. who was extremely supportive and professional. A special thanks to Maha Gaad for formatting the chapters and checking out references in case something was missing in action.

# 1 Education of Learners with Special Needs in the Gulf and the Middle East
## A Historical Perspective

In order to understand the core of any given educational system of any country, a known context consisting of an initial background will be required. Many Middle Eastern societies as well as the Gulf Corporation Council (GCC) countries are currently seeking inclusion of learners with special needs in mainstream education in their different ways despite a similar educational framework. This is an introductory chapter describing the general contexts and settings of the education system and the development of special education in the area from a comparative perspective among different GCC countries and some Middle Eastern countries. The chapter then explores the issue of inclusive education and examines the terminology used and the diversity of interpretation of such a controversial concept in the region.

## 1.1 A HISTORICAL PERSPECTIVE RELATED TO EDUCATING LEARNERS WITH SPECIAL NEEDS IN THE ARABIAN GULF AND THE MIDDLE EAST

The GCC members are as follows: the United Arab Emirates (UAE), the Kingdom of Bahrain (the smallest GCC country), the Kingdom of Saudi Arabia (the largest GCC country), the Sultanate of Oman, the State of Qatar, and the State of Kuwait. All are located on the Arabian peninsula in the southwest of Asia. Although there are differences between the social, political and economic aspects of member states (Table 1.1 shows relative size and population), shared similarities in cultural heritage stem from geographical location, a common language (Arabic) and a common religion (Islam). Each is differently impacted by modernization and certainly by the discovery of crude oil. The introduction and development of state education for all is one facet of that process (Benn et al. 2010).

Prior to examining the historical perspective related to educating learners with special needs in the Arabian Gulf and the Middle East, a brief background on the nine countries focussed on in this book will be outlined.

Table 1.1   Relative Size and Population of GCC Countries and Three Other Middle-Eastern Countries Examined in this Book as per 2009 Documented Data*

|   | Country | Land Area in Square Kilometers | Population as of Last Quarter of 2009 | Point of Major Expansion of Formal Education | Duration of Compulsary Education[1] |
|---|---|---|---|---|---|
| 1 | United Arab Emirates (GCC) | 83,600 | 4 million | 1970s | 9 |
| 2 | Bahrain | 711.9 | 650,604 724,645 | 1940s | 9 |
| 3 | Saudi Arabia | 2,250,000 | 19.9 million | 1970s | 6 |
| 4 | Oman | 309,500 | 2.33 million | 1970s | 9 |
| 5 | Qatar | 11,521 | 743,000 | 1950s | 9 |
| 6 | Kuwait | 17,818 | 1.576 million | 1940s | 9 |
| 7 | Egypt | 1,001,449 | 83,082,869 million[2] | first half of the 19th century | 9 |
| 8 | Tunisia | 163,610 | 10,486,339 million[3] | second half of 19th century under French occupation | 11 |
| 9 | Palestine[4] | 6,317[5] | 3.9 million[6] | | 10 |

*Some information in this table is retrieved from Benn et al. 2010.

Since 1981 the GCC has become a more collaborative enterprise as a political, economic, social and regional organisation, with scope to be jointly involved in economics, politics, security, culture, health, education, legal affairs, administration, energy, industry mining, agriculture, fisheries and livestock. It was established to meet the challenges imposed by the circumstances prevailing in the region, and to safeguard the welfare and security of its population which reached about 31,015,200 individuals in the year 2000 (Benn et al. 2010). In January 2008 there was a strategic move towards a more unified regulatory framework of co-operation between GCC countries: a GCC Common Market.

This recent unity has worked in favour of those making comparative studies of the region by making their task less daunting and unwieldy. In fact, it acted as a catalyst for taking this first look at the area of special education from a cross-country perspective.

The Gulf countries produce more than a quarter of the world's oil wealth and possess two thirds of all oil reserves. This wealth has enabled the Gulf countries to enter a new economic era. In the past the economy was dependent upon shipping, fishing and pearl-diving and, to a lesser degree, agriculture. The new era has brought with it important changes in both cultural and social structures which continue to impact on the lives of local people. These dramatic developments in various aspects of life began in the 1950s and accelerated throughout the 1980s as a result of the discovery of oil and subsequent related industrial development. Most of the changes were positive, such as the establishment of universal health and education services, and housing. However, this period was not without its problems and complexities, brought about mainly by the extraordinary speed, magnitude and diversity of change which profoundly affected the traditional way of life in Gulf societies (Al-Nakyb, 2001). There have been numerous social impacts including the enormous influx of foreign workers, largely from developing countries such as the Indian sub-continent into the development/infrastructure projects (Al-Harthi 1999; Al-Harthi & Al-Adawi, 2002).

Although examining the Gulf States is intriguing, it can, to a certain extent, be frustrating due to lack of literature and rapid change in decision-making in relation to education in general and special education in particular. However, though intent is present and often voiced, the actual path ahead appears to be less clear-cut. Shaw et al. (1995) stated that "a central problem for Gulf States' school systems is that while they are administered and relatively closely supervised by the local Ministries of Education, their activities do not take place within a coherent and explicit tradition of public policy." It is only quite recently, for example, that a committee has been set up in some GCC countries to develop the countries' educational policy whereas other Middle Eastern countries' educational systems have been long established; however countries experienced rapid change in a rather 'confused' shift from one policy to another following change of ministers and governments. When it comes to special educational needs (SEN), most countries have shown initiatives in beginning to address the need for laws to back intentions, with considerable urging from SEN activists and parent groups.

In the past few years, there has been a significant interest in inclusive educational practices in the Gulf and the Middle East. However, the interest in acknowledging and legalising the rights of persons with special needs in general and educational rights in particular, started long ago in the form of sporadic efforts.

Yet again, though, whereas SEN in the public school system of most Middle Eastern countries is gaining a foothold, within the private school system it is at a standstill—arbitrary SEN provision being dependent upon goodwill or business strategy options. The ideals and principles of inclusion cannot exist in isolated settings: To work legitimately, they have to be in the very fabric of the whole educational system of a country.

Looking at one example from the GCC, it is clearly stated in Article (12) of the UAE Federal Law No. 29 of the year 2006 for Special Needs Rights that "[t]he country assures equivalent education chances for the Person with Special Needs in all educational establishments, professional qualification, adult people education and continuous education. It shall be in the regular classes or in special classes." Article (15) states also that a Special Committee shall practice "putting of the executive programs to assure equal chances in education for special needs people starting from early childhood in all educational establishments in their all regular classes or in specialty units of education." Given this statement it should be apparent that provisions are available for the fairness and support of such pupils in the mainstream schools.

In reality, however, this is far from being accomplished. The researchers Gaad and Thabet (2009), following a 14-month funded nationwide study on inclusive education in the UAE which took teachers' views on suggested adoption of inclusion and reinforcement of the federal law, found that:

> The limited knowledge, recourses, training, and facilities resulted in high percentage of disagreement by the teachers about the proposed inclusion policy. The teachers in this study have raised concerns that in order to implement effective Inclusion in regular schools some important aspects need to be addressed. Teachers need more training in the field of special education, various special needs disabilities, teaching methodologies, and specialized people in this field to guide and assist them. The need to conduct training for teachers in different areas of disability is essential because currently there are no specialists available to provide such assistance in most schools. (Gaad & Thabet, 2009, p. 159)

The situation in relation to special education in some Middle Eastern countries is, however, somewhat different. An interesting contrast to begin with is Egypt, which despite its relatively high rate of illiteracy has the largest and oldest education system in the Middle East and North Africa. During the late 19th century in the Khedewi Ismaiil times, the first true interest in special education was shown by Doreek (head of inspection of schools section during the British occupancy) when he suggested the establishment of a school for the blind in 1874. The school started with eight learners (six boys and two girls). A proposal followed to establish a school for a hundred of those with disabilities in Egypt. The school was established, and 44 learners with visual impairment and 16 with hearing impairments were enrolled. Enrolment age was 9 to 12 for boys and 13 to 18 for girls. It was called the Deaf and Blind School but, unfortunately, it was closed in 1888 due to unknown reasons.

In 1900, a school for the Blind was established in Alexandria by a British woman, followed by another in the Al Zaytoon area in Cairo in 1901 which received donations from a Mrs Armitaj. In 1926, the Egyptian Ministry of Education (Al Maaraf) decided to prepare teachers for learners with special needs, thereby establishing a special department for teachers of the Blind in the teachers' college in the Bollaq area in Cairo.[7]

In 1927 primary education established classes for blind learners in a few primary schools and, in 1933, a Danish woman living in Alexandria built a non-government school for the deaf. During the same year, the compulsory education law was announced that gives all children the right to education. In 1939, the first government classes for the deaf were established: one in Cairo and one in Alexandria, being Egypt's two most populated cities. Demand was overwhelming and the Ministry decided to establish special schools across Egypt; so, by 1950, a vocational centre for Al Noor Schools for the Blind was established.

Education of those with intellectual disabilities followed and, in 1956, the first institute for such learners was established, accepting children with IQs of 50–70. Teachers for this establishment were sent to the UK for training. More special schools were opened in 1958 across the country with several hospital schools for terminally-ill learners. The first special education department was formally established under the name of "Department of Abnormal Children" with all the relevant duties for learners with special needs and disabilities. In 1956, the issue of terminology was taken into consideration for the first time in Egypt. As a result, the term 'blind' was substituted with 'visual impairment'; 'deaf and dumb' became 'hearing disabilities'; and 'intellectually disabled' was used instead of 'slow learner' or 'mentally retarded.'

In 1964, the sub-department of special education became an independent department. By 1970, the department had a head-in-charge and heads of sections for such units as planning and curriculum and teacher preparation.

On the 31 March 1978, Law No. 35 was issued to organize sections of the department as follows: Al Noor for the Blind was to become the Education Department for Students With Visual Impairments; Al Amal for the Deaf was to become the Education Department for Students With Hearing Impairments; and the Mental Department was to become the Education Department for Students With Intellectual disabilities (Al Tarbia Al Fekria). A fourth department for administrative services was also established. This subsystem of special education is the current one up until the present.

Another country in the region focussed on in this study is Tunisia. A recent surge of interest in inclusion can clearly be discerned by the rise in the number of 'integrative schools' that accept learners with disabilities and special needs. That number rose from 162 in 2004 to 265 in 2008. Likewise, the number of children included in compulsory education with such needs rose from 806 in 2004 to 1,134 in the 2009 academic year.[8] In fact, in the process of researching for this book, a top-ranking Tunisian decision-maker described Tunisia's inclusive policies as "developing by the day."

Alongside this general thrust towards educational emphasis, Middle Eastern governments have also been making a foray into special educational needs provision, in terms of their recognition of the need for a law to protect the rights of persons with special needs and disabilities. Egypt, as an example of a well established system, was one of the first Arabian countries to ratify the UN Convention on rights of persons with disabilities. However, it took time from the establishment of the first school for a category of special needs (School for the Blind in the late 19th century) to call for what is now known as the 'Education for All' trend. In a report published in 2004, the Egyptian Minister of Education, Dr Ahmed Gamal Al Deen Mousa, declares:

> Knowledge has become the point of development which plays the vital role of the existence of nations and the formulation of their future. Hence, the ability to provide education chances for all citizens, young and old, male and female, rural and urban, normal and with special needs no longer satisfies our educational ambitions, now we aspire to more elevated goal that is providing excellent education for all. (National Centre for Education Research and Development, 2004, p. 39)

In a similar vein, the Omani Ministry of Education declared on an official website that the:

> Special Education sector has progressed tremendously in the last two decades. The Ministry of Education is constantly providing the students with Special Needs with various types of facilities and services. In the first place it aims to provide the best programs, educational services, training and guidance to them in order to make them productive, integrated members in the society that goes in line with the needs and movements of this century.

And:

> The Ministry of Education provided various facilities and services to students with special needs to rehabilitate and prepare them to integrate in their society and participate to serve their country.[9]

Oman, like other Gulf States, has a relatively new education system (formal education did not start until mid-1970s). Special education in Oman is catered to by what are referred to as 'specialized schools.' There are two main establishments—Al Amal School for Hearing Impairments and Umar Bin Al Khadtab Institute—as well as programs for learning disabilities and programs for students with special needs (catering to gifted students mostly).

It is noted that the medical model to deal with special needs is still the trend despite claims of inclusion in the country. It is stated clearly on the official website that "[t]he students should be examined by a doctor before enrolling in the school."[10]

The attitude towards inclusiveness in the Palestinian Territory, however, differs appreciably. Despite being named a government priority, inclusiveness, perhaps not surprisingly, comes last on the list of resource prioritization in one of the most unstable areas on earth. Further details on such processes in Palestine will be covered in Chapter 2.

To conclude this section, one can argue that in most cultures nowadays, special educational programs, especially for young learners with special needs, have been well accepted by the public as an important part of the education system since the 1960s. Most of the Gulf countries, however, are relatively new and rather young nations in comparison to other Middle Eastern countries like Egypt. Therefore, educating learners with special needs has developed naturally following the development of formal systems of education in such countries. General consensus on the extent to which children could require special provision may have remained constant over the past three decades in most of the Middle Eastern and Gulf States despite calls for inclusion and governments' declarations of "caring for those with special needs." However, exactly what form this provision takes, who provides it, and when and where it takes place are issues which have remained highly controversial throughout this time period and are ardently debated today (Farooq, 2007, as cited in Kite, 2008).

## 1.2 DEVELOPMENT OF EDUCATION AND SPECIAL EDUCATION IN THE AREA

It is important to note that whereas 'special educational needs' has become a definitive buzzword in both the media as well as government policies, it is shrouded in mystery, in terms of both its implications as well as its actual workings. Information on the status of most of the GCC countries' current educational systems has proven difficult to find, as there is a dearth of accurate, up-to-date, reliable information in this area. Information specific to SEN is even harder to come by. Sufficient, clear documentation on SEN in the GCC would be reflective of focused, sustained effort in this field. Though the countries do have centres for children with SEN, details on provision for these children, as well as the children with SEN already in mainstream schools, are difficult to gather. Information on the exact range of services and expertise available is heavily dependent upon word of mouth, not a central information provider. The lack of basic information coupled with the obscurity of what SEN provision is really all about within such countries leaves the seeker bewildered by conflicting data.

If one looks at the development of education and special education in the area from a comparative perspective among different GCC countries and some Middle Eastern countries, there will be some challenges. The educational system in the GCC countries for instance, being relatively young, is fertile ground for research. Many avenues exist in terms of exploration, unearthing and recording. The challenge though is to embark upon study that is relevant to changing times and needs, and contributes to improving existing practice. Within such ideals lies the rationale behind this section.

The governments of most of the nine examined countries have placed educational reform, with special education as an important part of such a system, high on their list of priorities. For example, the UAE is aiming "to create an educational process that adopts world-class standards" (UAE Interact, 2007). The UAE is a rapidly developing country comprised of seven Emirates. "Rampant poverty in the various emirates . . . prevented the creation of a state education system until the beginning of the oil era . . . in 1971" (Talhami, 2004). Prior to this, "the level of illiteracy . . . was nearly 90%" (Talhami, 2004). As a result of this late formation and its previous hardship, the country has a relatively young education system compared to many Western countries. In order to create an education system, the UAE looked to more established systems for guidance such as in the US and the UK. Talhami (2004) claims that the country was "determined to reverse the tide of history by modernizing without totally yielding to Western prototypes and models of development." 'Pull-out' support (withdrawing special needs students from classes) was at its most popular in the US and UK during this time, and this could explain why the focus school uses this type of provision to support children with special educational needs; it was the system observed in the West and then replicated by the UAE in the focus school. The fact that the UAE did not want to "totally yield" could explain its resistance to full inclusion which is currently the popular model in the West for educating children with special educational needs (Spencer, 2009).

Reality, however, reveals otherwise despite positive calls for inclusion. One of the most relevant studies that reflect the cruelty of reality for some categories for learners with special needs is an unpublished master's dissertation by Farooq (2007) cited in Kite (2008). Farooq's thesis investigates the current status of educating Emirati children with autism spectrum disorders (ASDs) in Dubai. She focuses her study on local government schools and some centres in Dubai. Following her investigation, Farooq concludes that "a place for a child with autism in a public regular school in Dubai is virtually non-existent." She believes it may become possible in the near future, but at present most children "are either to be found in autism specific centres or all-purpose special needs ones." Furthermore, Farooq observes that the progress made by the children in the centres is uneven, with some hardly making any headway and others excelling in their developmental skills. At present, she continues, "although 'top-level' personnel have a 'positive air' about inclusion, administration and teaching staff are far more negative, believing mainstream school inappropriate for pupils with ASD" (Farooq, 2007, cited in Kite, 2008).

## 1.3 TERMINOLOGY FROM AROUND THE REGION

Currently, inclusion is a new concept in the still comparatively young and developing education systems of most of the countries discussed in this book. Possibly due to this fact, very few published studies involving terminology related to inclusion and/or the education of learners with special needs have been carried out in the region, and to the author's knowledge terminology related to the inclusion of learners with such needs has not been researched at all apart from brief sideline investigations by research postgraduate education students. This section is an attempt to examine terminology that is related to inclusive education that is currently used and the diversity of interpretation of the notion in the region.

Inclusion, although a broad concept which is often used interchangeably in literature with terms such as integration (Lomofsky & Lazarus, 2001, p. 306), can be simplified in definition as the right of each child to accessible education at their neighbourhood school by being fully included regardless of their disabilities, abilities, race, gender, nationality or any other factor (Friend & Bursuck, 2002, p. 4; Mittler, 2000, pp. 10, 11). Furthermore, Mittler clarifies that whereas inclusion refers to the school environment and its related components such as curriculum amongst others adapting to meet the child's needs, integration differs in that the onus is on the individual child having to adapt in order to "fit in" (p. 10). Inclusive schools therefore require their environment and system to adapt in order to accommodate all and any pupils enrolling (Lomofsky & Lazarus, 2001, p. 306).

Despite a relatively clear understanding of the concept of inclusion in many parts of the world, in practice it can be questioned whether many participants and stakeholders in the Middle East, particularly in the Gulf, who are working in the field of education have a clear definition and concept of what inclusion actually means, what it should entail and how it is to be applied. This could possibly be attributable to the fact that many races and nationalities live alongside the local people. The Emirates, as an example of a Gulf country, is settled by a diversity of cultural groups. In addition to the UAE nationals, there are various Arab groups, as well as Iranians, Filipinos, Indians and large numbers of Europeans and Americans. They are all known as expatriates (expats) and make up approximately 70% of the population. As might be expected, individuals' and or groups' concepts of inclusion tend to differ according to race, culture and background. Therefore, if a certain provision is offered by the government or the private sector to two peers in a primary school, their families could refer to such provision differently due to such diversity.

Hence, in such nations, inclusion remains a controversial term that has different meanings for different people. Terminology related to inclusion is very much related to learners with special needs that have developed in the region as more awareness of the impact of such terminology on people with special needs became apparent to the majority of people.

Special schools were once the popular choice for providing special provision (Spencer, 2009), and it is safe to say that most children with obvious and labelled special needs and disabilities are assumed to attend special schools in this part of the world. However, many government and non-government education providers have been strongly criticized for segregating children with special educational needs: "There is nothing that happens in a special school that cannot take place on a mainstream site" (http://www.csie.co.uk, cited in Flavell, 2001). Due to intense opposition, special schools are now out of favour, particularly since the rise of the inclusion movement. "The right of pupils with special needs to receive an education in mainstream schools has become a very significant issue in recent years" (Birkett, 2003, cited in Spencer, 2009). In this part of the world however, the story differs as, despite many scattered efforts and voices calling for immediate inclusion, and despite the support of legislations in many countries in the region, confusion still surrounds the controversial issue. This confusion is naturally interpreted in terminology describing such provisions.

Inclusion is seen as a part of an international phenomenon due to recent civil rights movements and global changes (Dyson, Gallannaugh, & Millward, 2003). The history of inclusion has been described as going from neglect in the early 20th century to segregation based on individual needs in the period 1920s–1960s and on to the present (Brusling & Pepin, 2003). However, Gaad (2004) indicated that some important changes have occurred since the 1960s worldwide which have influenced attitudes, treatment and expectations for people with disabilities. A widespread acceptance and support for raising children with disabilities now exists, and having them participate as part of the community is preferred rather than placing them in a special institute (Gaad, 2004).

In Egypt, for example, with the oldest subsystem of special education in the region, we find a natural move away from using insensitive terms to refer to people, particularly children, with special needs and disabilities. As mentioned in the introductory section, after years of using terms such as deaf and dumb, for instance, Law No. 35 of the year 1978 instigated more 'politically correct' terminology. This is even reflected in the choice of names of associated government departments such as the Education Department for Students With Visual Impairments and the Education Department for Students With Hearing Impairments. The most dramatic change was the renaming of the so-called 'Mental Deficiency Department' to the Education Department for Students With Intellectual Disabilities (Al Tarbia Al Fekria). As for inclusion, however, it is still vague and, with a lack of literature in the area, researchers are forced to look at a few references in articles that reflect the 'confusion' over the term inclusion and what it means exactly. It is presumed that social inclusion with provision of special classes in regular mainstream schools is used as inclusion. Partial inclusion is often used to refer to such units or classrooms inside the mainstream school. Many advocates, however, have reservations over combining the terms 'partial' and 'inclusion' as linguistically they do not match, because inclusion means including everyone and they see the use of such a phrase as sanctioning the continuing practice of exclusion, even if it means the students are within the precincts of the school.

The philosophies behind inclusion and integration should not be confused however. Within the recent right-based framework of education as a basis for societal progress comes the Salamanca Statement, which came forth at a conference organized by the United Nations Educational, Scientific and Cultural Organization (UNESCO) in 1994. Salamanca reminded governments that children with disabilities and difficulties were a part of the larger group of the world's children, and that inclusion and participation of all children were essential to human dignity and the concept of human rights. It also emphasized inclusive schooling to be a major player in the achievement of these targets, and advised governments to adopt this concept as law or policy, unless they were absolutely unable to do so. Inclusionists believe that a child's special educational needs should be met in the mainstream classroom along with his or her same-age peers in the nearest neighbourhood school (Spencer, 2009). Integration, however, is a term that is frequently used wrongly in this region to refer to inclusion. As explained by the Warnock report (1978) in the UK, integration differs from inclusion in that it enables a child with special educational needs to attend a mainstream school and receive the special provision that they need at the same time, regardless of where this special provision is provided. Integration could involve the child attending a special school part-time or a special class outside the mainstream classroom. "Integration was just one of a series of examples of the blurring of the rigid boundaries between special and mainstream education" (Clark, Dyson, Millward, & Skidmore, 1997).

The confusion also touches the provisions used to support learners with special needs in mainstream settings. In a mainstream school special provision can be made for a child by providing extra adult support. "Mainstream schools have long been expected to make provision for those pupils who have some special needs . . . through the provision of extra support" (Everard et al., 2004). The amount of extra support allocated to a child varies according to factors such as perceived need and the school's budget. The way in which this support is delivered is also subject to variation. Support can take the form of either 'pull-in' support, whereby an extra member of staff works with the child in their mainstream classroom, or 'pull-out' support which can also be referred to as withdrawal. During pull-out or withdrawal support, the child leaves the mainstream classroom in order to attend an alternative setting where the support is provided. This pull-out support is usually delivered by a special educator, qualified to help meet the child's needs, but the child could also be supported by a Learning Support Assistant. On occasions schools will employ such assistants because they are a cheaper financial alternative to a special educator, yet still provide the required 'support' for the child.

In a few of the countries studied in this book, whilst integrating, the child is given the minimum amount of support to ensure the experience is meaningful. Levels of support range from full one-to-one support in the mainstream class through to just settling a child in for the first few minutes of a lesson. Liaison is done between the support classes, the mainstream classes and home works to ensure that each child is provided with a broad, balanced and, above all, meaningful curriculum. In this case many refer to such provision as 'full inclusion' which in fact it is not.

Accommodation, modification and provision are often associated with the term inclusion, and this applies in this part of the world too. Issues related to strategies through which regular schooling becomes accessible to learners with special needs are a part of the concept too. However there is not much confusion about curriculum adaptation and flexibility to cater to differences in learning associated with such provision. As all the countries studied in this book use a federal rather than a central textbook based curriculum that is assessed at each school term through a written examination, any deviation from the federal textbook based curriculum is considered modification. Frederickson and Cline (2002, p. 81) have referred to a number of factors that contribute to successful inclusion of which appropriate curriculum is an important feature.

The term Learning Support Room is one of many used to refer to the setting where pull-out support is provided, and for most Arabic and Middle Eastern countries this option refers to a type of provision for what is known here as inclusion. Several additional terms for this model of service delivery include: the resource room (RR), the support for learning (SFL) room, and the special classroom. This term has been chosen as it is used on a daily basis in the focus school; therefore it does appear frequently throughout the papers and school documentation.

However, in much of the research conducted into this area of special provision, the term inclusion is preferred, but used not to reflect "all children regardless of their strength and weakness attending the neighbourhood schools with same age peers"; instead it refers to any form of social inclusion, or having the child in special units in mainstream schools. It is worth mentioning that the terms resource room and learning support room are interchangeable and refer to the same type of special provision. In addition, the term pull-out is widely used as synonymous with withdrawal throughout literature in this part of the world. This clarification is intended to eliminate confusion and provide the reader with greater clarity in an area where many are confused about provisions for learners with special needs in the region, and the terminology used to refer to inclusion of such learners.

In order to gauge the suitability of provisions, an understanding of different types of SEN is required. A critical evaluation as to whether certain difficulties are more 'includable' than others within school systems also needs to be considered in order to analyse the reasons for things being as they are at present. Therefore, terminology and labelling issues that are related to certain types of SEN are as important to examine. Currently, there are still issues with terms referring to certain types of such needs around the region. Due to openness caused by globalization, and many rights-based movements related to people with special needs and disabilities, many opt for more 'politically correct' and rather 'sensitive' terminology to describe such groups of people. However, in practice, and with all good intentions, many formal and non-formal terms are wrongly used to describe certain categories of special needs.

For the purpose of this book, the author collected documents, newspapers and even formal evidences such as school reports and communication to parents to arrive at a current situation on terminology used in relation to learners with special needs and disabilities and its effect on provisions and inclusion—or rather exclusion—from certain educational and social settings. The author also interviewed influential decision-makers on the same matter. People with special needs were also consulted. It was concluded that there is an apparent 'misconception' surrounding the term 'special needs.' Advocates in most countries called for differentiation between 'special needs' and 'disability,' as many people with special needs simply do not have disabilities whereas the opposite does not apply. Such generalization in the name of using more sensitive and culturally acceptable terminology caused further legal issues in the UAE: For example, the Federal Law No. 29/2006 was issued to protect the rights for persons with special needs, but many persons with disabilities initially found this intrusive, as they predicted that the pool of beneficiaries would simply become larger and could result in a lack of resources for those with disabilities who really needed such resources.

In Egypt, however, as well as Tunisia and Palestine, to avoid any confusion in the role played by authorities, a high committee, such as the Egyptian High Council of the Disabled, is concerned with citizens with disabilities. In the Gulf countries, however, the word 'disability' is often substituted, for all good and noble reasons, with 'special needs' which is now noted to have huge implications on provision including educational provisions and placement.

This also impacts on all categories, some being more affected than others. For instance, 'intellectual disabilities' are often confused with 'mental illness.' In an unpublished piece of research, the author found rather surprising results while undertaking research for an article on attitudes towards people with intellectual disabilities in one of the largest, most reputed universities in the Gulf region. In an attempt to test the hypothesis that people with intellectual disabilities are often confused for people with mental disorders, the researcher distributed a questionnaire asking final year undergraduate female students (mostly age 19–21) a simple question: Does having a low IQ (Intelligence Quotient) mean having a mental illness? The returned questionnaires were more than 400, and the analysis showed rather surprising results coming from a young, relatively well-educated group of people who consider themselves as 'pioneers' and 'revolutionaries': 26% of returned questionnaires answered "yes" to the aforementioned question, 64% said "no," 4% said "not necessarily" and the remaining 4% did not know the answer. Although it is not the purpose of this chapter to examine this particular research, as it was set for a different purpose and in different contexts, these findings gave some indication about social stigma associated with people with intellectual disabilities in the region. This is in line with Thomson et al. (1995), cited in Gaad (in press) in a recent study. Thomson et al. indicated that international studies have revealed the increased marginalisation of people with learning difficulties with the transition to adulthood; for example, a narrow range of leisure opportunities or workplace chances and continuing dependency on parents are factors often ignored by wider society (Thomson et al. 1995, p. 325). Gaad argues that the situation in the UAE is not any better than Thomson describes because until recently there was no discourse concerning intellectual disability. The segregation of those affected, by either keeping them closely confined to the home or, in a few cases, educating them in separate schools, meant that there was little acknowledgement of the existence of such people by the general public (Benn et al. 2010).

In formal documents the two main categories of disability are physical and intellectual disabilities with health impairments; whereas sensory impairments are understood to come under the umbrella of physical disabilities and anything to do with IQ deficiency is related to intellectual disabilities. In 2008, Dr Hanif Hassan, the then Minister of Education, stated in a formal presentation to a leading UN conference that:

> Something wonderful is happening to children throughout the United Arab Emirates. They are learning that all people are entitled to equal opportunities. They are learning to understand, respect, and appreciate people with physical or intellectual differences. (Gaad & Thabet, 2009, p. 159)

It is clear, however, that specific learning difficulties such as dyslexia (difficulties with reading, writing and recognising letters) and dyscalculia (difficulties with processing numbers and arithmetical figures) are 'lost terms' in this categorization. The two categories of special needs have their fair share of confusion too. An aspect that needs consideration is that dyslexia, for example, is a 'specific learning difficulty' that falls under the rather expansive umbrella of 'learning difficulties' or 'learning disabilities,' where many use the general term 'learning disabilities' to describe learners with dyslexia and/or dyscalculia, assuming that they have problems with their IQ rather than just a specific problem with one or more of the academic skills. Generalizations are often used, and the term is also comfortably used to refer to what is known in the Middle East as 'slow learners.'

On the contrary, international literature and formal organisations that look after such categories of people with special needs emphasize the strengths in individuals with dyslexia. According to the British Dyslexia Association, "Dyslexia is a puzzling mix of both difficulties and strengths. It varies in degree and from person to person. Dyslexic people often have distinctive talents as well as typical clusters of difficulties" (retrieved October 2009 from http://www.bda-dyslexia.org.uk).

To conclude, the terminology used to describe individuals with special needs in this part of the world is worth consideration as there is much miscategorisation or misuse of terms by the public due mainly to certain cultural and traditional factors. This has, unfortunately, meant that people with intellectual disabilities have been at the top of the list for being victimised and referred to insensitively. For the purpose of this research, the author has gathered evidence from everyday newspapers, and from media references in daily radio and TV shows which are a very effective means of communication in this part of the world. Terms like 'retarded,' 'backwards,' 'slow learners' and 'intellectually disabled' were noted, and, in one particular article the expired term 'Mongol' was even used to refer to the largest category of people with intellectual disabilities: those with Down syndrome.

# 2 Middle Eastern and Gulf Countries and the Quest for Inclusion
## Current Status and Learned Lessons

Many Middle Eastern societies as well as the GCC countries are currently seeking inclusion in different ways despite a similarity, to a certain extent, in the educational framework. This chapter describes analytically the way in which each state is approaching inclusion in its own current cultural and political practice.

## 2.1 THE KINGDOM OF SAUDI ARABIA

Saudi Arabia is the birthplace of Islam and home to Islam's two holiest shrines in Mecca and Medina. The king's official title is the Custodian of the Two Holy Mosques. The modern Saudi state was founded in 1932 by ABD AL-AZIZ bin Abd al-Rahman AL SAUD (Ibn Saud) after a 30-year campaign to unify most of the Arabian Peninsula. A male descendent of Ibn Saud, his son ABDALLAH bin Abd al-Aziz, rules the country today as required by the country's 1992 Basic Law. Following Iraq's invasion of Kuwait in 1990, Saudi Arabia accepted the Kuwaiti royal family and 400,000 refugees while allowing Western and Arab troops to deploy on its soil for the liberation of Kuwait the following year. The continuing presence of foreign troops on Saudi soil after the liberation of Kuwait became a source of tension between the royal family and the public until all operational US troops left the country in 2003. Major terrorist attacks in May and November 2003 spurred a strong on-going campaign against domestic terrorism and extremism. King ABDALLAH has continued the cautious reform program begun when he was crown prince. To promote increased political participation, the government held elections nationwide from February through April 2005 for half the members of 179 municipal councils. In December 2005, King ABDALLAH completed the process by appointing the remaining members of the advisory municipal councils. The king instituted an Inter-Faith Dialogue initiative in 2008 to encourage religious tolerance on a global level; in February 2009, he reshuffled the cabinet, which led to more moderates holding ministerial and judicial positions, and appointed the first female to the cabinet. The country remains a leading producer of oil and natural gas and holds more than 20% of the world's proven oil reserves. The government continues to pursue economic reform and diversification, particularly since Saudi Arabia's accession to the World Trade Organization (WTO) in December 2005, and promotes foreign investment in the kingdom. A burgeoning population, aquifer depletion, and an economy largely dependent on petroleum output and prices are all ongoing governmental concerns.[1]

> Saudi Arabia is a nation undergoing dramatic self-examination. Every aspect of Saudi Arabia's society and culture is being openly debated. We have recognized that a comprehensive, modern and open educational system—with new and revised textbooks—is fundamental to the growth and prosperity of our country. A thoughtful revision of this system is necessary, and indeed well underway.–(Prince Turki al-Faisal, USA Today, June 4, 2006)

### 2.1.1 The Executive Summary of the Ministry of Education 10-Year Plan 1425–1435 H ( 2004–2014 ), 2nd ed., 2005

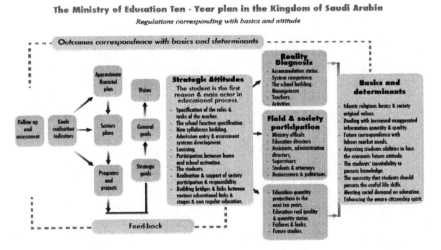

*Figure 2.1* The Ministry of Education 10-Year plan in the Kingdom of Saudi Arabia. From *The Executive Summary of the Ministry of Education Ten-Year Plan* 1425–1435 H (2004–2014), 2nd ed., by the Ministry of Education, 2005, p. 7.

## 2.1.2   Goals and Objectives of the Ministry of Education's Vision for the Next 10 Years

*Goals*

1. The education of 4- to 6-year-old children and the consideration of kindergarten as an independent stage in terms of its buildings and syllabi from other education stages.

   - To accommodate 4- to 6-year-old children (kindergarten stage) at a rate of 40% by the end of the plan.
   - To update the programs and activities on which early childhood education is based.
   - To supply kindergarten with specialized cadres to meet such stage classes at a rate of 10%.
   - To develop the programs and tools to measure children's preparedness for the preschool stage.
   - To develop a personnel preparation and qualification program at the kindergarten stage.

2. Accommodation of all age categories from 6- to 18-year-olds at various stages of education.

   - To make basic education compulsory.
   - To improve admission rates to an annual rate of 2% and to achieve accommodation of all male and female students by the end of the plan.
   - To secure the government's school buildings to accommodate the expected student population's growth to reach the rate of 90%.
   - To increase the number of male and female teachers at an annual rate of 3.5% according to the expected needs estimates.

3. Deepening the spirit of loyalty and pride of the country through intellectual awareness based on recognizing issues of the country.

   - Enlightening students with the challenges that face their country through a scientific and objective view.
   - Fixation the concept of temperance (mildness) other's respect, objective argumentation, and rejecting extreme views (ideas).
   - Enhancing the teacher's role in achieving the concept of national loyalty.

4. To prepare students academically and culturally at a local and international level to be able to achieve advanced posts internationally in the fields of math and science for the various age categories, taking into account international test standards.

- To enhance co-operation and exchange in cultural and educational fields between the Ministry and its international counterparts and establish the proper communication and administrative channels for such endeavor.
- To enrich the participation of the Ministry of Education in educational and cultural activities.
- To enhance the benefits of programs and projects by international and local educational organizations.
- To ensure the inclusion of international standard levels for students' academic (scientific) performance and for knowledge acquisition.
- To promote and facilitate students' participation in international math and science tests.

*Objectives*

5. To organize girls' technical education.

- To update the regulations and related systems in girls' vocational education and training.
- To increase the girls' education and vocational training by accommodating students at an annual rate of 30% in girls' technical education.

6. To develop the educational system for students with special needs.

- To develop educational programs for gifted male and female students in scientific and creative fields.
- To develop special education systems to correspond with contemporary international expectations and attitudes.
- To develop special education programs for students with disabilities.
- To secure the materials and proper educational environment for students with special needs.
- To increase teachers' vocational development to fully prepare them to work effectively with students with special needs.
- To increase the opportunities for the development of the special categories of education shared with the private sector.
- To expand society's participation in protecting the rights of children with special needs.

As is apparent from the preceding, students with special needs were included in the plan (point 6 and its sub-points). Such a point was incorporated into what is known as the 'Inclusion Project' in the Kingdom.

## 2.1.3    Official Activities in Saudi Arabia With Regards to the Inclusion Project

The Inclusion Project[2] is applied in many Saudi schools and it has two categories; one is partial inclusion, where students are included in special classes in regular schools; the other is full inclusion where students are included in regular classes and are provided with other services, such as resource centres, traveler teacher program, consultant teachers and special education programs.

Providing education to gifted and special needs students is considered one of the main objectives of the education policy in Saudi Arabia. Moreover, the Ministry recognizes the challenge of having 20% of students in regular schools in different countries that need special education services, and by providing these services, not only will those students benefit from them, but the educational process in the school system in general will be affected as well.

To achieve this goal, a new educational strategy was put into place via regulation for students with special needs. There are many aspects to it:

- Creating more special classes based on two categories: one for students with mental speech disabilities using a special education based curriculum; and the application of the same regular curriculum in special classes for students with visual and hearing impairment.
- Using various teaching systems, such as a program of special education classes, resource centres and traveler teacher programs for gifted children and students with physical, visual and hearing disabilities as well for students with emotional and behavioural disorder. Bearing in mind that the main reason that Saudi is applying the Inclusion Project in its schools is to enhance the special education level, not to judge its success or failure, as well as to provide educational services and to meet the needs of each student with special needs.

Many regulations and frameworks have been set up for effective inclusion, such as limiting the number of students in each class that has students with special needs to not more than 25 students; conducting continuous training for school staff before and after the Inclusion Project and clarifying to them the main objectives of the Inclusion Project and its requirements.

Furthermore, there are 223 programs and institutes for the Inclusion Project that are as follows: cognitive development institute, learning disabilities programs and institutes for students with hearing and visual impairments.

Many schools provide educational services for students with learning disabilities in resource centres in government schools. Moreover, the country is seeking to establish a big project for gifted students, which will have two stages: The first stage identifies or discovers gifted students via certain assessment tools; the second stage provides services and educational and social care for them by using the facilities and services of the resource centre after school and then preparing special individual plans for them.

In addition to this, special programs will be prepared for students with certain behavioural issues within the framework of special education services.

### 2.1.4   Attitudes of People in the Kingdom of Saudi Arabia (KSA) Towards the Inclusion Project

As any newly established system, the Inclusion Project has had its fair share of interest among the Saudis. Some have claimed that including students with special needs in regular classes would be a potentially successful experience that would need the support of families and social associations,[3] and they have called for more support for this pioneering project; others, however, have watched carefully and wondered to what extent this would work, especially with a divided boy/girl system and the huge geographical area that must be covered.

Dr Abdulla Al Husain, Executive Director of Special Education in the Ministry of Education in 2008, stated:

> Including students with autism, mental, hearing, physical and hearing disabilities in government schools as well as providing special programs for gifted students is considered a unique experience and matured educational vision towards preparing students with special needs to be productive people in the society.

Having said that, the Ministry of Education considers including these students in regular schools a vital element in the development of the society, since they were previously isolated from the community and had no proper opportunity in education. Hence, it is important now to integrate them in the school system and the society so people will get used to socializing effectively with them as well as allowing them to participate in the community as other citizens. Therefore, the Special Education Department in the Ministry prepared various educational facilities for them, such as building special classes in regular schools that follow other classes.

Al Husain argued that the Ministry started applying the Inclusion Project after reviewing successful experiences of the countries that have applied it, such as Sweden and the United States. Moreover, it conducted its own research in Saudi Arabia by forming a team of Specialists in Special Education, Supervisors and Teaching Staff of Special Education from King Saud University to study the Project prior to applying it. The research included 29 elements in its examination of the school environment; it set up proper assessments and examinations based on individual differences; and it also assessed curriculum programs related to Arabic and math. The findings of the research approved the success of the Inclusion Project, and it included many educational recommendations to achieving it.

Dr Naser Mousa—a well-respected scholar who is known as 'the father of special education' in the Kingdom—wrote the following in Arabic on the most important advantages and disadvantages of the Inclusion Project:

### The advantages:

1. Regular schools are considered the natural environment for both children with special needs and regular children to grow together after providing the required arrangements to meet the academic, social and psychological needs of the children with special needs.
2. The Inclusion Project allows the children with special needs to stay with their parents in their homes for the entire schooling period which allows them to become productive members in their society and on the other hand, their parents can fulfil their obligations towards them.
3. The Inclusion Project is considered a flexible education facility that can develop, increase and provide various educational services to students with special needs. Moreover, it provides opportunities for educational associations to benefit from this experience and eliminate the provision of education to certain categories.
4. The Inclusion environment contributes to the increase of social acceptance of students with special needs by their regular peers and provides opportunities for social integration. It also helps them to imitate and learn their peers' behavior by communicating with them.
5. Early inclusion of students with special needs with their regular peers contributes to the enhancement of their perception towards each other, working to create a social environment in which regular children can get rid of their limited? perceptions about special needs people.
6. The Inclusion Project works to create a real environment where children with special needs get exposed to various experiences that lead them to develop real perceptions about the world that they live in.

### The disadvantages:

1. The Inclusion Project requires the development of a strong and supportive system that prepares the teachers and demonstrators in Special and Regular Education to meet the basic needs of children with special needs. These requirements are important to provide opportunities for them to practice their social and academic activities effectively in regular schools. Moreover, if in the event of any failure in the application of this system, both students with special needs and regular students would be affected negatively, as well as society in general.

2. Negative perceptions of some regular class teachers and parents of regular students contribute to negative outcomes of the inclusion educational experience in schools.[4]

## 2.1.5 Activities Related to Inclusion in the KSA

Due to many factors, the main category of special needs recorded in the Kingdom is learning disability. The Conference to Counter Learning Disabilities in Saudi Arabia was organised to highlight its importance and to look at how the inclusion project would support students with learning disability in the Kingdom.

Over 1,000 participants and 44 international and national speakers attended a 4-day International Conference on Learning Disabilities in Riyadh to develop a system, which could impart better education for Saudi students with learning disabilities.[5]

Prince Ahmed Bin Abdul Aziz, Deputy Minister of Interior, opened the conference at King Faisal Hall on Sunday. The conference was divided into a number of workshops and seminars with papers presented by some of the best international speakers from America, Europe and other Arab and Gulf countries.

Nassir A. Al-Mosa, Supervisor-General of Special Education, Ministry of Education, and organizer of the conference, said the event is very important since the Kingdom has established a system called "resource room program or RRP" which caters to the special education needs of the students with learning disabilities. He said around 5% of the 4 million students in Saudi Arabia have learning disability and need special education, and that the number of RRPs first established in 1995–1996 has increased from 12 to 1,226 in 2006.

Al-Mosa stated,

> Saudi Arabia is the first country in the region to have pioneered by establishing special education for students with learning disabilities. Learning disabilities are a spectrum of disorders affecting people who have no sensory or mental deficiency by definition.

He continued: "Dyslexia or inefficient reading is the most common learning disability among those diagnosed with the disorder," He went on to say, "Children with learning disability are classified as neither physically nor mentally handicapped." And further, "The learning disability is a behavioural disorder manifested by a significant unexpected specific and persistent difficulty in acquisition and use of efficient reading, writing or mathematical abilities."

However, the public schools in Saudi Arabia don't isolate students with learning disabilities from the normal students. All students attend the same classroom; however, students with learning disabilities will be sent to attend an RRP for special education. "There are teachers, who are specialized to teach students with learning disabilities," Al-Mosa said.

He went on to explain that the major thrust is to achieve a 100% success rate in imparting special education to the students with learning disabilities, which currently falls short of covering all 5% of students in Saudi Arabia. According to international standards, the percentage of students with learning disabilities is 5%. "So," according to Al-Mosad, "in the case of Saudi Arabia the percentage is not alarming except we want to provide RRP to all students with learning disabilities." He said this is the first international conference on learning disabilities hosted in Saudi Arabia. After the deliberation in workshops and seminars conducted during the 4 days, the conference will pass recommendations "and that will be transformed into projects to achieve better results in the future in this area."

## 2.2   THE KUWAITI EXPERIENCE WITH INCLUSIVE EDUCATION

This part explores the famous, better-known, leading Kuwaiti experience with inclusion. It examines the critical effect of inclusion on the lives of Kuwaiti learners with special needs in a country that was the first to issue a designated law to regulate and protect the rights of persons with disabilities in the Gulf area, and that was in 1996. Article 16 of the Kuwaiti law established the Higher Council for Disability Affairs (HCDA). The article states that the HCDA is to be formed with a president and 11 members. Interviews with the head of special education at the Ministry of Education in Kuwait (November 2008) revealed that this was to ensure that the HCDA plays an important role and is formed from various parties that represent people with disabilities and is headed by the Minister of Social Affairs or his or her delegate. The 11 members including the president are divided into government and non-government representatives. Six of such 11 members must be government representatives (one minister, three under-secretaries of states, the head of the General Social Affairs Agency and a representative from Kuwait university). The university member of staff ranking, however, was not identified in the law. The remaining members come from non-government organisations (NGOs) that represent people with disabilities in Kuwait.

Article 6 of the Kuwaiti law regulates homes and rehabilitation services for those with profound and multiple disabilities. stating that [t]he country must insure provision of rehabilitation and workshops as well as hostels for the necessary cases of people with disabilities."

As for the educational rights for people with disabilities however, Law No. 49/1996 actually stated that "educational and cultural provisions should be offered for those with disabilities according to their mental and physical needs" (Article 3).

## 2.2.1 Assessment of Current Situation

Kuwait currently follows a system where learners with similar disabilities/impairments (with respect to spectrums across disabilities) receive their education/rehabilitation provisions in separate schools directly under the management of an educational subsystem represented by the special education department that is part of the Ministry of Education, not as previously under the Ministry of Social Affairs.

The model is simply classic exclusion and categorization based on disability. There are 15 schools catering to the following categories and segregated according to disabilities (source: interviews with principals):

1. Al Ataa KG (currently hosting 25 learners)
2. Al Noor (boys, primary) for learners with visual impairments
3. Al Noor (girls, primary) for learners with visual impairments
4. Al Noor (boys, middle and secondary) for learners with visual impairments
5. Al Noor (girls, middle and secondary) for learners with visual impairments
6. Al Amal (boys) for learners with Down syndrome
7. Al Amal (girls) for learners with Down syndrome
8. Al Tarbia Al Fekria (boys, primary) for learners with intellectual disabilities and hearing impairments
9. Al Tarbia Al Fekria (girls, primary) for learners with intellectual disabilities and hearing impairments
10. Al Tarbia Al Fekria (boys, middle and secondary) for learners with intellectual disabilities and hearing impairments
11. Al Tarbia Al Fekria (girls, middle and secondary) for learners with intellectual disabilities and hearing impairments
12. Al Rajaa (boys, primary) for learners with physical disabilities
13. Al Rajaa (girls, primary) for learners with physical disabilities
14. Al Rajaa (boys, middle and secondary) for learners with physical disabilities
15. Al Rajaa (girls, middle and secondary) for learners with physical disabilities

The author visited four schools as suggested by the Department of Special Education. A series of interviews, some of which were taped for reference, were held with the principal of each school and a selection of teachers (those observed in their classrooms by the author and a representative from the Ministry of Education PR department). The visited schools were as follows:

1. Al Rajaa (boys, primary) for learners with physical disabilities
2. Al Rajaa (girls, primary) for learners with physical disabilities
3. Al Rajaa (boys, middle and secondary) for learners with physical disabilities
4. Al Rajaa (girls, middle and secondary) for learners with physical disabilities

A typical visit to a school would include an introduction to the head teacher/principal about the purpose of the visit and the number of observations and interviews required to be undertaken. A guided observation for 15–20 minutes in three different subject areas followed, with interviews with the teacher concerned to confirm services offered. The author used triangulation (using more than one method to collect data to ensure validity).

Provisions are offered with slight modification in assessment and some methods of delivery, however the main national curriculum is adopted except for in schools for those with intellectual disabilities. Speech and language therapy, as well as physiotherapy, are offered in most schools, and teachers are highly skilful and multi-tasked.

Social inclusion programmes, for example: 1-day integration in regular schools, visits to museums, and open days at schools are adopted by most schools to raise awareness. However, no serious attempt towards inclusive education took place in the government sector.

## 2.2.2 Issues Related to Inclusion in Kuwait

Interviews with participants showed that educating learners with special needs and/or disabilities meant to many people "providing full-time education for those with disabilities," and inclusion was not part of the equation. Despite several cases scattered across the regular schools, there was hardly any real inclusion going on. By the end of the visit, a clear picture of the services offered to learners with one category of special needs (physical disability) was well-established.

Kuwait, however, provided schooling for most disability categories at both primary and secondary level. For secondary age learners, Article 14 of Law No. 49/1996 stated that "rehabilitation provision and vocational settings should be provided for those at the appropriate level at state expense."

The research visit for the purpose of this chapter showed a clear lack of confusion over the term 'inclusion.' Whether they were in mainstream regular schools or not, it did not really matter. Inclusion ('Al-Damj' in Arabic) was not known to the majority and, despite being the first to issue legislations related to disabilities, no development has occurred since the 1970s apart from changing some of the titles of the schools to more 'politically correct' terminology. A good example is changing the institute of physical disability formally known as 'institute of paralysis' to Al Rajaa (which means desire or hope). Education for those with disabilities and special needs means to many simply provision of educational services in segregated settings. The segregation is on various levels: age groups (primary and secondary), gender based (boys and girls), and disability based where school goers with similar disability were schooled together.

## 2.3 THE STATE OF QATAR

In this section, Qatar's scattered, but well planned, pilot inclusive experiences are examined in light of the latest, yet controversial educational reform. It is worth mentioning that such a distinguished system for inclusion would never be where it is today without the help of a very dedicated high profile royal, Sheikha Hessa Khalifa A. Al Thani, who worked tirelessly to advocate for issues related to disability rights in this small but confident Gulf estate. The country indeed has leaped forward in providing services for learners with disabilities following her election for three terms (each term is for 3 years) as UN Special Rapporteur that started in 2003 and ended in 2008. In her words, "This role as UN Special Rapporteur and this engagement has changed me. I feel proud of this change. It has given me a wider vision of the society. I have a better understanding about human rights."[6]

### 2.3.1 Special Education in Qatar

Education for children with special needs started in 1974 with the opening of a single classroom affiliated with a boy's primary school. By 1980, the number of classes rose to three, supervised by eight teachers. In 1981 Al Amal (meaning 'hope') Institute for Boys was opened, to be followed by the opening of Al Amal Institute for Girls.

Students attending these schools receive Islamic education lessons to be good citizens and to help them grow physically, mentally, emotionally and socially. Such schools provide students with knowledge and necessary experiences suitable for their specific situations.[7] Talent nurturing is considered an important area of the system. To cater to talented, gifted and creative students, the Ministry of Education set up the Centre for the Talented and Gifted in 2001 to provide activities, programs and services which would help such students develop and refine their capabilities. The Centre aims at helping educational institutions design educational services and put them into practice in order to serve gifted students. The Centre also aims to carry out research and academic and experimental studies on the concept of talent, creativity, talented students' needs and means of supporting their special needs.

## 2.3.2 The Inclusion Project and the Qatari Education System

Including students with special needs in regular classes is an achievement to be proud of by the government schools in Qatar. The term 'inclusion' was not foreign to the ears of educators and family members in the State of Qatar; however, it entailed establishing special classrooms in regular schools where learners with special needs and/or disabilities were socially included with their peers during assembly, break time and some extra-curricular activities, but they spent most of the day in a segregated classroom known as 'the special classroom.' Fatma Al Aryth, Special Education Specialist, states that:

> Every child has the right to education and should be provided with an acceptable level of education based on the recommendation issued by the Special Education Committee on 29th March, 1986. The Committee recommended to apply the Inclusion Project, prepare special classes for students with special needs because they are important members in the society. Having said that, this report will discuss the outcomes of the Project after applying it for 18 years, with regards to whether it was successful, to what extent it has achieved its goals and what are the future plans for the Ministry regarding the Inclusion Project?[8]

She added that from 1979 to 1980 the Ministry organized a committee to run and manage the inclusion program under the name of 'Special Needs Care Association,' and that they were responsible for identifying disability conditions in schools, supervising students with special needs and establishing private institutes outside the country. In 1992, the Ministry applied a partial inclusion strategy for students with learning disabilities in regular schools with their peers in coordination with UNESCO by conducting training and workshops to provide them with the required skills to deal with students with special needs effectively.[9]

The Ministry supports special education and the Inclusion Project by specifying a budget to send many teachers for training in the field of special education to Al Khaleej Al Arabi University. The Ministry grants approximately 12 scholarships each year to major in a higher diploma to teach students with learning and/or mental disabilities and gifted students with the budget of 36,000 Dinar yearly. There are also 105 teachers working currently in government schools holding master's, higher diploma, and bachelor's degrees in special education.

The Ministry spent 9,508,002 Dinars for furniture and school equipment in 48 schools. It also specified budgets to spend on school facilities for students with special needs, such as preparing stairways, elevators, toilets and special classes with equipment for students with minor mental disabilities.

As for the curriculum, a committee was organized consisting of special education teachers that had experience working in inclusion schools, curriculum specialists and a representative from Al Khaleej Al-Arabi University to develop proper curriculum for students with Down syndrome and minor mental disabilities. The committee's task was to consider individual differences in education and meet their abilities in order to enhance them. Hence, it was decided to prepare curriculum for arabic, math, music, computer and physical education (PE) subjects that includes preparing their prewriting and calculation skills. In addition to that, the program focuses also on teaching them important social and life skills to build their self-esteem and independence so as to be able to integrate in the society. Currently, the Ministry has included 6,000 students with special needs in 84 schools and they are as follows:

- Students with minor mental disabilities
- Students with Down syndrome
- Students with hearing and speech disabilities
- Students with physical disabilities

Currently, the Ministry is applying three types of Inclusion Programs in schools: disability programs, learning disability programs and gifted programs. The school program has been spread over 5 days in schools where the students study 25 lessons weekly with five lessons per day, and they are in the following subjects: Islamic, Arabic, social studies, math, science, social and independent skills, art, music and PE.

The program also provides guidance and medical facilities from a special team consisting of a paediatrician, psychologist, special education teacher and social worker. It provides motivating learning tools, different teaching strategies, speech therapy and medical services. The program focuses on raising awareness in schools and conducting training workshops for school staff by coordinating with specialized universities in Bahrain and Al Khaleej University.

Regarding the challenges that faced the project, Ms Fatma commented that very few understood and cooperated with the objectives of the project despite the awareness campaigns. An unclear vision of the project's objectives, and huge age differences for some students (the range was 14 to 16 years old) led to many behavioral problems among some of the students. Furthermore, some of the medical reports for students were inaccurate which resulted in admitting students with false reports. To overcome these challenges, the special education teachers conducted a series of interviews with activity teachers, parents and students with special needs to introduce and explain to them about the project and the services it provides as well as to raise awareness about the characteristics of students with minor mental disabilities and Down syndrome students to provide guidance to them on the different ways of dealing and communicating.

As for the activities, the schools enrolled students with special needs in many national and religious activities, including participating in school programs and competitions between different schools, engaging in schools' morning assembly programs and taking them on scientific and entertaining outdoor visits.

As for students with learning disabilities, the schools had to identify their reading, writing and mathematical disabilities, and provide enhancement programs for them according to an individual differences program.

It was noted that this conference clarified that the Inclusion Project is considered as being against isolating and discriminating any person because of his/her disability.

Shikha Al Masouri, principal of Mosa bint Muhamed School, commented:

> With regards to students with learning disabilities, the schools offered many services and facilities for them, such as providing special lessons in Arabic and English subjects. They also provide academic services in learning resource centres to enhance their learning ability. ("The Independent Schools Present Advanced Teaching Model," retrieved [Day Month Year] from http://www.sec.gov.qa/content/resources/ detail/2286 June 2009)

The objectives of the learning disability program are to identify students that face learning disability through a series of individual assessments and to prepare educational plans for each student separately based on their needs and abilities. The program also provides consultancy services to parents to raise awareness and help their children to take advantage of their skills and monitor the progress of their performance in regular classes.

Ms Reem Al Derham, learning resource centre specialist, argued that:

> The resource centre in Moosa Primary School aims to enhance students' logical thinking and skills through different learning resources that are available in the centre such as using technology, internet to encourage students to research and investigate which will result in building students' self esteem.

Moreover, because the learning resource centre is equipped with learning tool equipment, reading sections and researching tools, the students look forward to visiting it and use most of the resourses to enhance their skills, abilities and self-learning.

Under the heading Selecting Six Model Schools to Include Students With Special Needs, Dr Thabia Al Suleyti presented a paper entitled "Learning Disabilities in Qatar Between Challenges and Achievements" at the Aeyn Shams University on 10–11 July 2008.[10]

In her introduction she argues that *the right of learning* was agreed upon by all religions. UNESCO has considered it as a vital right for every individual despite his/her disabilities. Qatar's policy has approved support and care for individuals with special needs with regards to providing opportunities to learn and based on the 'Child's Right' agreement in 1995, article (23), and legislation No. 53 for the year 1998. One class was opened in a government school in 1975 for students with hearing and speech disability. In 1991–1992, a centre for psychological and communication consultancy was opened to provide care and service for students with behavioural and psychological issues, and for students with speech and learning disabilities.

Dr Al Suleyti explained that the special education aims to identify and monitor students to focus on his/her psychological, social, cultural and economical status in order to provide the required care. Furthermore, in 2002–2003 many direct services were provided to schools with regards to the Inclusion Project, such as preparing a team consisting of psychologists, speech therapists and physical therapists to assist students with learning and speech disabilities. Prior to this Project, these students were not being identified or perceived as regular students and were labelled as stupid and careless students, which led to high numbers of drop-outs from schools.

She added that the Inclusion Project is based on including students with special needs in regular classes by preparing the required learning atmosphere to achieve equal opportunities and encourage regular and special education teachers to support this project.

### 2.3.3 The Inclusion Project: Take 2

The Inclusion Project that started in 2003–2004 (which differs from what was previously known as the Inclusion Project that started in 1986 which meant simply enrolling learners in special classrooms in mainstream schools) started by including 80 students with physical and learning disabilities in two primary schools by providing supportive services and resourse rooms. Then, in 2006–2007, more students were included in different levels till grade six where another five schools were opened to accept students with physical and learning disabilities.

Dr Al Suleyti also explained the reasons behind learning disabilities, and ways of identifying students with reading disability (dyslexia) which is considered 80% of the learning disability cases. She emphasized the importance of identifying the students and preparing individual plans to enhance their skills based on individual abilities.

She also talked about the learning centre that was established in 1996 by his Highness Shiekh Hamed bin Khalifa Al Thani, which is part of Qatar's Science and Society Development Association. This centre offers educational, medical and consultancy services to students with learning disabilities by enhancing their skills and abilities to reach its maximum level.

Then, she mentioned the importance of raising precautious awareness to young people before getting married and educating them about the causes of delivering children with learning disabilities and ways of preventing these disabilities.

After identifying all students with learning disabilities in primary government schools, the project prepared plans in two stages: the first involves raising awareness via media lectures, programs and brochures that targeted teachers, social workers, school administrators, principals and parents; the second involves collecting all diagnostic information and enhancing programs and forming a team consisting of specialists and social workers to prepare individual progression plans for students with learning disabilities.

As for the roles of the special education team, she said that they are responsible for assessing students in the resourse room; identifying the level of disability; chartering a history of the condition via their school records and developing individual progress plans after parents' approval. Then the specialists will divide the students into groups based on the level of their disability, where each group should not exceed five students. Moreover, there should be a fixed schedule such that each student should take two lessons weekly in a subject in which he/she faces difficulties.

Finally, Dr Al Suleyti recommended issuing regulations for students with special needs to provide them with opportunities to learn in a healthy environment; linking the curriculum and the testing system with students' abilities; as well as developing flexible curriculum to meet their needs and enhance their skills to discover their potential.


## 2.4  SULTANATE OF OMAN

Officially, the Sultanate of Oman is an Arab country in southwest Asia on the southeast coast of the Arabian Peninsula. It borders the United Arab Emirates on the northwest, Saudi Arabia on the west and Yemen on the southwest. The Omani inclusive practice is determined by many factors, especially in rural areas where geographical challenges can act as obstacles on the way to implementing inclusion.


### 2.4.1  Special Education in Oman

The special education sector in Oman has progressed tremendously in the last two decades. The Ministry of Education is constantly providing the students with special needs with various types of facilities and services. In the first place, it aims to provide the best programs, educational services, training and guidance that goes in line with the needs and movements of this century to them in order to make them productive, integrated members in the society. The Ministry of Education provides various facilities and services to students with special needs to rehabilitate and prepare them to integrate in their society and participate to serve their country.[11]

The Ministry of Education prepares different programs for students with special needs and provides rehabilitation programs according to their abilities and based on planned programs to integrate them into society.

Special education provisions are offered in mainstream schools, which is a relatively new trend, and in specialized schools. Such specialized special education schools are as follows:

- Al Amal school for hearing impairments
- Umar Bin Al Khadtab Institute
- Programs for learning disabilities
- Programs for students with special needs
- According to the official Ministry of Education website, the educational objectives for schools are as follows:
- To provide educational services and academic skills for students with hearing disability according to their abilities and level of performance.
- To integrate students with hearing disability into the society and communicate with them as regular individuals.
- To raise awareness in the families of students with hearing disability about the causes of this disability and educate them with proper ways to deal with their children.
- To build self-esteem in students with hearing disability and help them to accept their disability by enhancing the relationship between them and their society.
- The conditions of accepting students in Al Amal School for hearing disability are as follows:
- The schools accept students from age 5 to 8 years old, and others may get admitted who are older by up to 2 years, if there is any vacancy.
- The IQ should not be less than 70.
- The students should be examined by a doctor before enrolling in the school.[12]

## 2.4.2 Provisions and Modifications for Learners With Special Needs

The following are the provisions offered to learners with one category of special needs according to the Omani education system:

1. Preparation stage: This is for 2 years until the students learn the pronunciation of letters and words via hearing aids. It is effective in the case of both severe hearing loss and those with minor hearing disability. They also provide education through using different tangible and visual teaching facilities to link the word with its picture.
2. Primary level:

   - Grades 1 to 4
   - Grades 5 to 10
   - After primary grades 11 to 12, students study the curriculum for primary level after being modified and adopted based on the abilities of students with hearing disabilities.

The responsibilities of the Special Education Department are as follows:

- Issue general policy for special education and gifted students' sector.
- Prepare programs for special education for different categories based on the general policy.
- Identify cases and conditions of preschool students with special needs that need to be provided with special education facility by coordinating with educational zones.
- Provide qualified human resources to work in the special education field.
- Provide educational facilities and equipment for various types of special education programs.
- Coordinate with educational zones to benefit from the creativity of gifted students and enhance their abilities.
- Provide training for school staff.
- Coordinate with different educational zones to provide activities and programs that help to discover students' abilities and gifts.
- Supervise special education programs in schools.
- Modify and develop special education programs.
- Prepare programs and plans to send special education students to private institutes and specialized schools outside Oman.
- Prepare awareness programs for parents by coordinating with educational media sector.
- Prepare a budget for activities and special educational programs.[12]

### 2.4.3 Omani Inclusion Program for Students with Special Needs

According to the Omani press, the Ministry of Education started applying the inclusion program for students with special needs in primary schools:

> The Ministry of Education prepares to launch the first Inclusion program for students with Special Needs in Primary Schools across the nation. The program will first be applied in two educational zones (Al Batinnah and Al Dakhelia) in four categories; of these, two of them will be dedicated to mental disabilities and the other two to hearing disabilities by providing all the required educational facilities according to the types of disability. (*Samail-Oman*, Oman Newspaper, 16 September 2005)

The Suroor Primary School in Samail Province held an educational meeting with Mr Khalifa Al Qasabi, the director of the Special Education Department in the Ministry of Education, and many educational staff to discuss the Inclusion Program.

Mr Al Qasabi confirmed that two classes would be opened in Dakhelia Province, one of which would be in Nizwa (Madina Al Elm Primary School) with 14 students (boys and girls) with hearing disabilities from 6 to

13 years old. The other class would be in Suroor Primary School in Samail for students with mental disabilities, with 13 students (boy and girls). Both schools would start applying the program by the following Monday.

After that, Ms Raya Al Ajameia, chief director of the Special Education Department, spoke about the importance of following up on the Inclusion Program in the schools to make sure of its success and identify the type of facilities for disabilities available in the Al Wafa Centre before registering the students and enrolling them in primary schools. She emphasized the importance of having continuous follow-up by the school principal, teachers and advisors as well as raising awareness inside and outside the school. She added:

> The department of special education has set up specific goals and objectives for students with special needs that they should be included in primary and general school, in order to provide them with opportunities to be integrated into the local society. It is important to raise the awareness in society about the importance of taking care of people with special needs and providing all the required facilities outside Muscat, the capital of Oman, because the Ministry aims to prepare those students to become regular students in a school environment. Hence, the success and failure of this first project in Oman is related to the people that apply it if they are convinced of its success. Moreover, the schools should treat these students as regular students and include them in various educational activities supervised by the school itself.

In addition to that, Ms Suad Al Fory, special education supervisor, said:

> This program is considering the first project across the nation, and it is considered a humanitarian service before its educational service. Therefore, social workers and teachers in schools should cooperate and make this inclusion project a success and include students with special needs in different school activities such as morning assembly programs etc.

She added:

> The Ministry will conduct different training for teachers to teach them how to deal with students with special needs and apply different teaching strategies. As for the curriculum, the same regular curriculum will be applied with students with hearing disability; whereas, the curriculum for students with mental disabilities will be different for primary level. It will depend on individual planning for each student, for example, a regular lesson that is designed to be delivered in one day for regular students, may take a week or more for students with mental disabilities.[13]

Looking at another inclusion experience, Ms Aysha Al Balushi, principal of Al Nazaer Primary School in Al Battinah, Oman, presented a report of inclusion experiences of students with special needs in primary schools. She explained about the different types of inclusion, of which one is complete inclusion in which the student with special needs gets included in regular classes with regular students, studying the same curriculum. However, this type of inclusion requires that the students have the ability to be enrolled in regular classes by taking into consideration the various types of educational approaches, such as the Traveler Teacher Program, Consultant Teacher Program, Resource Rooms and Special Education Classes.

The other type is partial inclusion which involves preparing separate and special classes for students with special needs to be provided with special types of educational facilities and care. It also provides opportunities for them to participate in some class and non-class activities as well as to benefit from other school facilities.

Social inclusion—which is the simplest type of inclusion—involves students with special needs not being included in regular classes with their peers; instead, they are included in other school activities, such as trips, camping, art and sport activities.

She added that the Inclusion Project is a global view to integrate students with special needs in their community with their peers. Furthermore, she mentioned that the inclusion project was accomplished with success in 2005/2006 only in primary schools in Muscat Province, and many other provinces were deprived of these services due to the high cost of the project (seehttp://www.dged.net/modules.php?name=News&file=print&sid=662).

There are prior steps that should be taken into consideration before applying the Inclusion Project, and they are as follows:

- Identifying students with hearing and mental disabilities from 6 to 11 years old.
- Selecting schools that are prepared and have approved standards to enroll students with special needs by coordinating with educational zones.
- Specifying certain conditions to accept students with special needs with regards to the level and degree of their mental, hearing and visual disabilities.
- Organizing a committee to select students with special needs and enroll them in schools based on the specified admission rules.
- Providing training for teachers and school staff to prepare them for the Inclusion Program.
- Preparing school students by raising awareness to welcome their peers with special needs among them.
- Preparing instructional and guidance programs for parents of students with special needs and non-special needs.

- Identifying the classes that are intended to be opened in each school by considering the following elements:

1. Avoiding isolation of special classes from regular classes by providing required learning equipment.
2. Reducing the number of students in those classes to 6 to 12 in each class, and locating the classes on ground floors to meet the needs of students with physical and mental disabilities.
3. Not labeling or identifying those classes with special signs or boards because the core objective of the inclusion project is to eliminate discrimination between regular students and those with special needs by raising awareness about considering individual differences between children.
4. Specifying the roles of school staff, teachers, social workers, students and individual skills development teachers and parents with regards to the Inclusion Project.

The Inclusion Project recommends working on building and developing self- esteem in students with special needs by meeting their psychological needs to enable them to integrate and participate effectively in society as soon as possible. The project also aims to provide continuous guidance, training and consultation to school staff and students to discover the abilities and gifts of those students in order to encourage them to participate in activities across the nation by providing all the required facilities for them.

In conclusion, she added that it is important to raise the awareness in the community, and to develop and accept the inclusion concept as part of our culture to quicken the success of the inclusion project by distributing brochures, providing lectures, conducting parent meetings and holding awareness campaigns. Furthermore, the Inclusion Project and rehabilitation program are considered human investments that have economic and social effects.

## 2.5   THE KINGDOM OF BAHRAIN

Bahrain, despite being considered a small GCC country, has a big inclusion agenda. The education system in Bahrain started in 1919 with the establishment of a school for boys (Alhedaya School in Al Meharaq), followed by a school for girls, in 1928. Previously, people used to send their children to places called 'Katateeb' which were traditional houses in which the Quran (the Muslims' holy book) was taught.

In 2006, there were 125,842 learners in 205 government schools in primary, elementary and secondary levels, as well as 61 private schools.

The education system in government schools has developed in the past few years based on the government's vision that "education is most effective in helping face life's challenges" (Ministry of Social Development, Bahrain,

2006). The Special Education Administration in the Ministry of Education is responsible for identifying and monitoring students with special needs in government schools and colleges, whereas the Ministry of Social Development is in charge of the overall service provision for people with special needs and disabilities.

The country began what is known as the Inclusion Programme in 2005. The Ministry of Education aims to apply the Inclusion Programme by including students with special needs in regular classes based on certain modules and conditions. Such conditions as stated in the report are:

- Includes students with physical and visual disabilities in regular classes as regular students. As a result of this program, many students with special needs joined regular classes, graduated and now are enrolled in higher education in universities and colleges.
- Includes children with Down syndrome and other mental disabilities in special classes in 22 schools. The project is in the process of extending to other schools.
- Partially includes students with mental disabilities from rehabilitation centres in some lessons such as art, PE and social activities. Furthermore, students with minor mental disabilities are included in regular classes in government schools.
- The Ministry of Education works on developing the skills of its human resources in the field of special needs by granting them scholarships to get higher degrees and master's or bachelor's degrees in special education.
- The Ministry of Social Cultivation works on developing its employees' proficiency in the rehabilitation and care centres by granting them scholarships to majors in special education studies via programs offered by the Arabian Gulf University. Thirty teachers joined the program from many rehabilitation centres.
- The Ministry of Health, Education and Social Cultivation provides training to their employees in special needs fields to cooperate together to make this project a success.
- The Ministry of Education works on involving parents of students with special needs that are included in government schools to participate and share their expertise to hasten the inclusion process and the students' integration into society. Moreover, it holds many awareness campaigns for the parents of students with special needs in schools.
- The Ministry works on modifying the curriculum and prepares plans based on individual differences for students with special needs to meet their abilities.
- It includes students with hearing disabilities in regular classes by providing required hearing equipment to facilitate their participation in the class.
- Includes students with physical disabilities in regular classes, to be taught similarly to other students and to participate in social, enter-

tainment and sport activities. The school works on offering them opportunities to participate in art and other competitions as well.

- The Ministry of Education has made many adjustments to school buildings by preparing stairways, special toilets, specially equipped classes and elevators to facilitate their movements in the school.
- Since 2001 many students with mental disabilities have been included in regular schools through specialeducation classes and by providing them various educational programs that they need such as modified curriculum based on individual differences.
- The Ministry of Education uses a new learning strategy for students with visual impairment via "The Travel Teacher" and special education specialists by coordinating with the Saudi Institute for People With Visual Impairment.
- Provides facilities for students with visual impairment such as books with large fonts, and coordinates with the Saudi Institute to borrow enlargement equipment for classes.
- Assigns specialized therapists such as speech therapists as special education teachers in government schools to rehabilitate students with speech or hearing disabilities.

The centre model is the adopted model for learners with disabilities, whereas learners with specific learning disabilities (dyslexia, dyscalculia, etc.) may have a chance in the regular education system but segregated classes are referred to as special education classes. As described in the *Bahrain Report on Special Needs* (Ministry of Social Development, Bahrain, 2006),

There are special education classes in government schools for students with learning disabilities. Furthermore, the administrators work on discovering other special needs cases in schools such as visual, hearing, speech and mental disabilities and transfer them to specialized centres.

The definition of people with special needs in the Bahrain Regulation No. 74 for the year 2006 with regard to their rehabilitation and employment was identified based on all international regulations and agreements. The definition of international agreements for people with special needs is: "that people with Special Needs are those with long-term physical and mental disability that prevents them from performing regular life activities properly and efficiently in society like their peers" (Ministry of Social Development, Bahrain, 2006).

The definition of special needs in the Bahrain Regulation No. 74 for the year 2006 is as follows:

A person with Special Needs is one who suffers from some weakness in his/her physical, mental abilities due to sickness or accident or a genetic element that has caused partial or full inability to work or to continue working and progressing in life. As a result, he/she needs to be provided with the required rehabilitation to be integrated into society again. (2006 Bahrain regulation, section 74)

Although primarily the business of people with special needs and disabilities in the country is related to the Ministry of Social Development, the philosophy of the Education Ministry has been to integrate special needs children into mainstream schools where possible, but for children that require specialist care there are the facilities and resources available. The Special Education Unit within the Ministry of Social Development was established to coordinate the welfare and education of children that require special assistance (Bahrain Brief, Gulf Centre for Strategic Studies, 2001).

The publicised percentage of people with disabilities compared to the population in 2006 is 1% (2006 Bahrain regulation, section 74). The percentage is obviously considered contrary to the international estimation of which the number of people with disabilities in the world is about 10% of the total population. The justification for this rather low percentage which appears in the same report is as follows:

1. There is a high standard of health in Bahrain, due to every individual in the Kingdom being provided with all types of services, including primary and secondary medical services.
2. Highly developed awareness in Bahrain means people are more cautious and thus prevent accidents and avoid sources of danger.
3. The awareness of the concept of good nutrition, living a healthy lifestyle and avoiding bad quality food which might cause sickness has increased among people of Bahrain.
4. There is a cooperation between formal and informal organizations to spread awareness in the society regarding preventing accidents and injuries which might cause lifelong disabilities.
5. Early diagnosis for preborn children and providing required services that could prevent disabilities in the first stage of the pregnancy are standard.
6. Early diagnosing and providing medical services are standard.
7. There is a high percentage of educated parents, resulting in improving their awareness regarding proper parenting and health care of their families (2006 Bahrain regulation, section 74).

Bahrain's reputation in the Gulf for caring for children with disabilities was referred to in the country's own report on people with disabilities:

> Bahrain's reputation in the Gulf for caring for disabled children saw it chosen as the location for a regional centre for the teaching of the blind, the Saudi-Bahraini Institute for the Welfare of the Blind. It

provides educational, training and cultural programmes in addition to health, social and psychological care for sight-impaired boys and girls. The Institute uses the same grade structure and curriculum as the regular state schools and after 14 years of age the students are transferred to secondary schools, which provide them with specialist assistance. (2006 Bahrain regulation, section 74)

The government of Bahrain states that it considers the rights-based approach when dealing with members of the public with special needs and/ or disabilities.

The Constitution included that "all people are equal as humans and dignity. All the citizens have equal rights and the same general obligations by law. There is no discrimination among citizens whatsoever based on race, ethics, language and religion" (Kingdom of Bahrain, Constitution, 2002).

Bahrain issued certain regulations to protect the rights of people with disabilities in the country and they have developed over the years to reflect the country's commitment to people with special needs and disabilities. The Constitution of Bahrain issued a regulation in the year 2002 that

[E]very citizen is entitled to educational and health services in the country by providing medical care and establishing different types of hospitals and health organizations. Furthermore, every citizen is entitled with working opportunities in public sectors according to the country's' regulations. (Kingdom of Bahrain, Constitution, 2002)

Bahrain has a Human Rights Committee that carried out consultations with the United Nations High Commission for Human Rights on the teaching of human rights studies. In his own words, the Minister of Education stated in September 2006:

We have discussed with United Nations High Commission for Human Rights representatives—who were here to attend the Awareness Development of Human Rights Workshop—on the provision of a working team to train Ministry of Education teachers on how to integrate the principles of human rights in all subjects. (2006 Bahrain regulation, section 74)

It is clear from the country's own report on people with special needs and disabilities—"the support of the Ministries for people with special needs and disabilities in local special needs centres"—that the services offered to such individuals in society are rather seen as a rehabilitation-based support and has only one aspect that focuses on the Inclusion Programme in schools. The support as stated in the constitution could be in the following areas:

- Applying the inclusion program by enrolling students with special needs in schools.
- Developing and enhancing the abilities and skills of the employees of the centre by conducting training and workshops.
- Financial support to cover the required expenses of the centres, such as the salaries of the employees.
- Providing license to many schools and private organizations.
- Granting lands to build the centres.

The interest expanded beyond initial education as a life-long, rights-based approach, defined the rights of such people in employment and acted as a tool of empowerment to secure independence. Bahrain joined the Arabian Agreement No. 17 for the year 1993 for rehabilitation and employment of people with special needs and disabilities according to Regulation No. 3 for the year 1996 and is still committed to empowerment of people with special needs and disabilities.

The current local labour regulation indicated ensures and maintains the required social insurance, medical services and social services for all citizens in the case of working disabilities. In 2006 another regulation was issued, No. 74, which was about "holding vocational training, employing people with disabilities and providing constant and organized medical, educational, vocational, transportation, sport enrolment, housing facilities and other services." It also emphasized the important role of the Ministry of Social Development to establish vocational centres, workshops and accommodation for people with severe disabilities who require special care.

Bahrain signed the UN international convention on Rights of Persons with Disabilities in 2006, and the Ministry of Social Development participated in its meetings that discussed the draft of the convention before its publication in the eighth session which was passed by the General Assembly later on in August 2006.

Quota-based obligatory employment of people with Special Needs and disabilities is the current policy adopted in the kingdom of Bahrain. Regulation No. 11, from the rehabilitation and employment of people with special needs regulation, emphasized that employers should employ Bahrainis with special needs in their workforce if they have 50 employees or more, whether they work in one place or in different areas within the same corporation. The number for obligatory employment of people with special needs is decided based on the percentage that the Higher Committee of the Ministry of Labour specifies which is considered not less than 1–2% percent of the total number of employees.

To conclude, integration of learners with special needs and disabilities in regular school is also seen as an activity related to Bahrain's commitment to the rights- based approach in health, education and social justice. However, the rehabilitation, not the education, and the centre-based approach, not the school-based one, is still the current model of offered services.

## 2.6   EGYPT

Egypt was a natural target for occupation for thousands of years by many invaders for its strategic geographical location, natural resources, population and, lately, its political status among the Arabs. This section looks at the slow moving inclusion process in times in which many Egyptians are struggling with their daily needs.

### 2.6.1   Egyptian Special Education System and Current Provisions for Learners With Disabilities

There are several offered forms of provisions that accommodate learners with disabilities in Egypt, however such provisions are mostly category-based. Schools for the those with mild intellectual disability with IQs of 50–70; schools for the blind and those with visual impairments; and schools for the deaf and those who are categorised as 'hard of hearing.' This is in addition to the old special classrooms in mainstream schools. Such schools are government funded common day-care centres known as 'special schools' that are designed to cater to the majority of children with disability in a catchment area. Typically, one would find one of those in every major city and town, whereas villagers with disabilities must commute to the nearest town or city to attend the school. Such schools are helping to provide some form of individualized education to learners with disabilities who are lucky enough to be enrolled in the mainstream system. However, some may debate the effectiveness of such schooling in preparing the individual with disability to blend in and be included in society where all types of people are interacting. The long-standing argument that 'children that learn together learn to live together' is missing and, therefore, social problems may be encountered later down the line outside of the school gate and in life after the school years. It is not easy to find accurate statistics but there is a sense of 'pride' about the number of government special schools. On an official website, it is claimed that

> The Ministry of Education pays due attention to this category. Statistics show a stable increase in number of students and classes in 2005/2006 are as follows:

- Number of schools reached 804.
- Number of classes reached 3,929.
- Number of students reached 36,808.[14]

In the case of full inclusive schooling the scenario differs somewhat. Shenouda and Al-Agha (2009) claim that

> [T]here are currently very few children with special needs who have joined mainstream schools as the concept of inclusion and support

services have not been disseminated in all of the schools in Egypt. Hence, at present, inclusive schools have only accommodated a limited number of children with mild or moderate disabilities (who represent around 70 percent of children with disabilities in Egypt, p. 36).

This, in their view, is due to various reasons such as the *limited number of teachers* qualified to teach in inclusive classrooms, as well as a *lack of trained assistants*. Relative *'newness'* of the inclusion concept and the tendency of schools to accept only the easiest cases, as well as the physical inaccessibility of schools to accommodate children with mobility disabilities, was also blamed for the small number of learners included in Egyptian schools (Shenouda & Al-Agha,, 2009, p. 37).

Research for this chapter showed that referral to special education and classification of any given child are the most important procedures in the school life of a child with disability in Egypt. A child is usually referred to a special school based on the following: one result of IQ tests carried out in health insurance clinics for children with learning difficulties; recommendations of diagnosticians and physicians; and/or refusal of schools to accommodate students as well as, in some cases, family's concern or anxiety or their inability to teach the child.

Interestingly, when Mrs Sahar Khaled Al-Agha, technical director and program planner, The Friends of a Bright Tomorrow Association for People with Special Needs, Cairo, Egypt, was asked, "Can all children attend inclusive schools?" she replied,

> In my opinion, not all students can attend inclusive schools; a child is considered eligible if he/she meets the following criteria:
>
> • He/she is of the same age group as other able-bodied students;
> • He/she must be autonomous enough to meet his/her basic needs (i.e., going to the bathroom on his/her own);
> • He/she must be chosen by a competent, specialized committee apt to determine his/ her capacity to cope with and adapt to the curricula.
> (Shenouda & Al-Agha, 2009, p.37)

Such views are in line with others expressed by Egyptian participants from the field of special education more than a decade ago when Gaad (1989) investigated perception towards inclusion of certain categories of disabilities into mainstream Egyptian schools. The similarity indicates that the whole notion of inclusion is not quite understood, especially with respect to its 'unconditional' access to all children to the neighborhood school with their same-age peers.

If one looks at the criteria for classification, one finds that abilities and capacities of a child may be classified; psychologists make use of a number of tests, such as IQ and educational attainment tests, adaptive behavior examinations as well as visual and hearing measures to do this. However, according to the SETI[15] Centre for Advice, Studies and Training in learning disabilities, children must not be labelled or identified in terms of education or participation in society. Thisis in recognition of the infinite diversity of characteristics that people possess: Therefore, people "classified" under the same category do not necessarily share all its attributes (Shenouda & Al-Agha, 2009, p. 35).

## 2.6.2 The Pilot Inclusive Project in Egypt

In order to test to what extent inclusion would be feasible in Egyptian government primary and elementary schools, a pilot project was funded by UNESCO in collaboration with the Ministry of Education.

> According to Nagib Khozam, SETI Centre director and professor of education psychology at Ain Shams University, "the pilot was implemented in 15 elementary and primary schools, the latter all public, in collaboration with UNESCO and Save The Children Egypt, with approval from the Ministry of Education." It involved teacher training, support groups and various facilitation programmes, as well as a campaign to raise awareness among children and staff. And the result? Inclusion is feasible, and will have a positive impact on both special-needs children and their peers.[16]

Looking at other views from a parental perspective, Dina, the mother of a 5-year-old with Down syndrome, sees that to change attitudes and pave the way for societal reform, children are the place to start. She argues that misunderstanding, fear and pity—these sentiments, born of ignorance and linked to age-old assumptions about ability, normalcy and human potential—persist, and no one has figured out an effective approach to changing them. Furthermore, Egypt lacks a successful inclusion model. Nowhere can children with and without special needs meet on an equal footing, in a place intended for both equally. Children with special needs attend special needs schools where they are pampered rather than taught to care for themselves. Lifelong dependency, even in simple tasks like feeding or dressing, is the result. Egyptian law disallows school-based inclusion of children with special needs in the classroom, and teachers are not equipped with the requisite understanding to be helpful. Doctors, too, lack the understanding they need to prepare parents to help their children learn. Everyone involved needs education and information and exposure.[17]

## 2.6.3 The Egyptian Call for Inclusion

Lababidi (2002) argues that

[D]espite declarations of the rights of the mentally challenged and the disabled, in 1971 and 1975, respectively, the inclusion move is relatively novel throughout the world. At the local level, children with disabilities are provided for under the 1996 child law and the first and second decades for the Protection of Egyptian Children (1989–99 and 2000–10), neither of which has granted the right to inclusion. Though the current child law (under amendment and discussion at the Shura Council) grants education for all children, some articles limit those with special needs to special education. Hence, the whole matter is left to the principles' [*sic*] choice of convenience. So far, primary, preparatory and secondary students with disabilities continue to be legally subject to the whims of school principals, unless they attend one of three types of specialised schools in Egypt, as defined in *Silent No More*.

Media sometimes gives an indication of where a certain country is heading with regards to a certain topic or issue. In *Al-Ahram* (the most popular daily national newspaper in Egypt) and under the title "Inclusion Call" in its weekly online issue dated 28 June 2007, Amira El-Noshokaty reviewed a plan to include children with special needs in mainstream primary schools in the busy, so-called 'never-sleeping' capital, Cairo. She illustrates her point through the story of Amr Ashour, 14, who likes school and enjoys the company of his fellow fifth-year students despite his difference from the majority of them. According to his elder sister Safaa, given Amr's condition—which has trapped him in a toddler's body and keeps him more or less stationary, the whole time—this was not always the case. The nearest special needs school was too far to be a practical option, and when he was finally registered at his present private primary school, Amr was frequently mocked and bullied. The principal has managed to control the situation, however; so much so that Amr is now not only academically, but socially top of his class. But to get to the present position, Amr's family had to go through an expensive 2-year battle.[18]

Many advocates who are calling for inclusion are puzzled at the fact that in such a large country, people with disabilities fail to obtain their 'right' of inclusion in the mainstream school. According to the same newspaper, there are some 2 million school-aged children with special needs, of whom only about 50,000 get their fair share of education. The figures were cited by Nabil Sisostres, network coordinator at the Together for Family Development (TFD) institution, speaking at a recent conference on the subject, which called for the inclusion of children with special needs in mainstream schools. Founded in 2003, the TFD includes over 13 NGOs specialising in special needs: "There are some 7.5 million people with special-needs in Egypt, and if you count the concerned parties—with four to a family— that makes 30 million, 10 million of whom have the vote. Just imagine the power they could wield," explained Sisostres.

They need not be legally and socially marginalised, in other words. And sure enough, in the last few days (Sisostres stated this back in 2007), the government has permitted the admission of students with "mild disabilities" in elementary and primary schools throughout the country—the first step in a 5-year plan of the Education Ministry starting in the school year 2007–2008—reflecting the success of pilot projects implemented by the Support Education Training for Inclusion (SETI) Centre of CARITAS, an eminently commendable step[19].

To conclude, there are no doubts that Egypt, despite some awareness of the importance of inclusion and some calls from professionals and advocates, has a long way to go when it comes to inclusive education. Shenouda and Al-Agha (2009) in their "Can Special Needs Education Institutions Contribute to Inclusion?" argue that, in their views and arguments, "Inclusive education should be the rule instead of the exception" (p. 34). They based their call for immediate inclusion on one simple fact: that is, the capacity of provisions in an over- populated, under-resourced country.

> In the early 20th century, Egypt embarked on setting-up special education schools for children with intellectual, hearing and visual impairments. Years later, these schools still have limited capacities to accommodate around 38,000 children (or less than 2 percent of children with disabilities in the country) as reported by the Special Education Department. Thus, we, in line with the United Nations Educational, Scientific, and Cultural Organization's (UNESCO) recommendation, believe that the best way to attain the Education for All (EFA) objective lies in making regular schools into inclusive ones. (Shenouda & Al-Agha, 2009, p. 46)

Reality, however, may be as optimistic as this view. Lababidi (2002) states that:

> [T]hose under the ministry's jurisdiction do not accept students with an IQ lower than 50, and they teach a simplified version of the curriculum, while those for the blind and the deaf follow the regular curricula using Braille and a mixture of sign language and visual aids, respectively. In effect, the ministry caters to no more than four per cent of the disabilities with which Egyptian children are afflicted.

In addition, a recent study by TDF found that for no convincing reason, learning disabilities, speech impediments and dyslexia, autism, social and psychological issues, physical disabilities, multiple disabilities and brain injuries resulting from accidents are not officially attended to.

## 2.7   TUNISIA

The educational and social care of people with special needs and including them in different educational aspects are not considered new directions for the educational and social policies in Tunisia. Best known as Green Tunisia among its Arab and North African countries, Tunisia was the first African-Arab country to ratify the UN convention on the rights of persons With disabilities and commit to an inclusive policy.

### 2.7.1　Inclusion in Tunisia: A Historical Perspective

According to figures and numbers presented by a chief inspector for schools, Mr Ali Baator, at the International Arab Conference on Rehabilitation in 2007 on the history of inclusion in Tunisia, since the 1970s, many children with special needs were able to join regular school through automatic inclusion without any private prior commitment, and the numbers of such learners were as follows during the school year 2006–2007:

- First stage of primary education: 4,195
- Second stage of primary education: 1,157
- Secondary education: 833

Furthermore, this strategy supported students from the 1991–1992 school year based on the president's concerns to further support children with special needs who are included in regular primary schools. As a result, three schools were assigned in every state of the republic for complete inclusion with the co-operation of authorized associations.

During 2003, and like many other countries, the Tunisian government has prepared a national strategy for the complete inclusion of children with special needs in regular educational institutions since their childhood with the help of authorized associations, at least at the first level.

Therefore, this strategy and the action plan is prepared by the joint executive, technical committee that consists of four ministries and representatives of related associations and was called 'The National Committee for School Inclusion.'

#### The General Goal:

To ensure the complete inclusion of children with special needs in regular schools gradually:

- The first stage: 2003–2004/2005–2006
- The second stage: 2006–2007/2010–2011
- The third stage: up to 2015

#### Specific Goals:

- To work on enhancing the level of school systems to include children with special needs.

- To develop the capacities of related parties in the inclusion program.
- To ensure positive enrolment of all related parties in the educational process directly or indirectly through an integrated media plan.
- To improve the co-ordination between the responsible people from the government sector and associations.
- To support the early educational inclusion opportunities, especially at the preschool stage.
- To work on preparing the required environment and overcoming financial obstacles to ensure complete integration for every individual with special needs in general life.

## 2.7.2   The Tunisian Inclusion in Schools Project

The Tunisian project known as the 'Inclusion in Schools' project has considered supporting people with disabilities, protecting them, and including them in vocational, cultural and educational intermediates as a national responsibility that concerns the individual, family, country and the society. Furthermore, different types of inclusion represent the basic foundation for the strategy that the Tunisian government has depended and bet upon. Many regulations and programs were prepared to support the inclusion program for children with disabilities based on equal opportunities.

The principles of the school inclusion program are based on the international rights-based best practices such as:

- Slamanque (Spain, 1994) recommendations on principles, policies and practices that concern people involved in disability education.
- "Education for all" plan (Dakar, 2000) and the international plan "Good Quality Education for All, Vision 2015."
- Recommendations of the Regional Arabian Conference which was held in Beirut in 2001. It discussed the importance of compulsory primary education, free of charge, and of including students with special needs in the education system.
- On the national level, the principles of the school inclusion programs were based on the following plans and policies:
- "Schools for all; everyone should have the chance to learn in school" from the statements of the dialogue of the future presidential plan.
- The instructive policy for the school education on 23 July 2002.
- The Action plan for the 'School of Tomorrow,' 2002–2007.
- The instructive policy to support and protect people with special needs in 2005.

The Inclusion Program started during the school year 2004–2005 and was able to include 299 children with special needs divided spread over 111 schools in the first year of primary education in all the Republican states. They were as follows:

- Physical disabilities: 60
- Hearing impairments: 75
- Mental disabilities: 138
- Other disabilities: 26

The aforementioned numbers according to gender were:

- Female: 119
- Male: 180

### 2.7.2.1   The Action Plan and Achievements of the Project

1. *Regulations that support the project*: the policies, rules and decisions related to people with special needs to educate and include them in schools.

   ◦ The instructive regulation for school education, Regulation No. 80, issued on 23 July 2002.
   ◦ The instructive Regulation No. 83 issued on 15 October 2005 was related to supporting and protecting people with special needs.
   ◦ The presidential program for Tunisia 2004–2009 was related to assist the progress of the inclusion program.
   ◦ The presidential decisions related to opening special sections for the preparation year for children with special needs (July 2004), circulating these sections gradually and expanding the number of schools for inclusion (November 2005).

2. *Preparing proper school environment (accessibility matters)*:

   ◦ Reporting the planned arrangements in the 'school project' for the benefits of the included children with special needs in schools.
   ◦ Three children with special needs are to be included in one section as the minimum number of inclusion in schools.
   ◦ Preparing individual pedagogy program if required.
   ◦ Providing technical equipment.
   ◦ Details of preparation:
   ◦ (140) passage ways/ramps for physical accessibility to, and inside schools
   ◦ (103) multi-resource room
   ◦ (151) medical transportations and pedagogical equipments

3. *Training*:

   ◦ Training 48 inspectors, 24 doctors and social workers

4. *Media and communications*:

   ◦ Conducting interviews with media specification for 1 to 3 days in summer 2003.

- Developing and applying the announcement plan for the benefits of all the related parties of the school inclusion process starting from the school year 2005–2006.

5. *Accompanying children with special needs in regular schools*:

- Providing pedagogical and medical care for children with special needs based on the individual educational plan (educational, vocational training, associations and social workers).
- Dedicating 2 hours by an assistant every week to support students with special needs in the specified sections where they were included.

6. *The new role of associations and specialized centres following moving learners to inclusive schools*:

- Providing the required facilities and other services to inclusive schools.

7. *Evaluation and follow-up*:

- A study for school inclusion situation in Tunisia (Handicap International, 2004).
- Media and communication strategy (Handicap International, 2005).
- Follow-up and evaluation studies conducted by the General Inspection Committee of the Ministry of Education and Training starting from the school year 2004–2005.
- Yearly accomplished field and administration follow-up studies from 2004 by the General Directory of the first stage of primary education from the Ministry of Education and Training.
- Accomplished regional workshops and seminars conducted by the National Committee of School Inclusions on December 2005–2006.
- The program has achieved the following quantitative results during the school year 2006–2007:
- The number of prepared schools for inclusion: 221
- The number of schools that applied for or opted for the inclusion program and admitted students with special needs: 201
- The numbers of included students with special needs were as follows:

 * First year: 241
 * Second year: 268
 * Third year: 249
 * Fourth year: 227

- Gender-wise the numbers were as follows:

* Male: 584
* Female: 401

○ The numbers of each category of disability were as follows:

* Physical disability: 155
* Hearing impairment: 279
* Mental disability: 469
* Multiple disabilities: 82

○ The number of schools that acquired preparation section for inclusion: 51
○ The number of children with special needs in the preparation year: 75

*Learners' results*: Progress and failing percentages for the school year 2005–2006 is considered one of the indications of the program success:

○ The progress percentage from Year 1 to Year 2 was 86.30, whereas the failing percentage was 13.70.
○ The progress percentage from Year 2 to Year 3 was 86.85, whereas the failing percentage was 13.15.
○ The progress percentage from Year 3 to Year 4 was 93.77, whereas the failing percentage was 6.22.[20]

Looking ahead, it appears from the quantitative and qualitative progresses which were presented earlier, that the inclusion program of children with special needs in regular schools has achieved an important aspect of the planned goals in spite of its early stages. However, according to interviewed participants in the field of special and general education, as well as decision-makers on the national project, there were some challenges in the way, and they are as follows:

○ Delay in applying the announcement plan with all its aspects.
○ Difficulty in circulating and applying the individual educational program.
○ Lack of training, especially the practical training.
○ Therefore, the following points are considered the most important goals of the next stage which were approved by the Higher Council of Education in Tunisia:
○ Providing good educational quality for children of special needs in regular institutions according to their disabilities.
○ Providing early preschool education for children with special needs, and proper training to participate in the success of the program.
○ Improving mindsets and views in order to involve different parties in fulfilling the goals.

## 2.8 INCLUSION IN THE WAR ZONE: A PALESTINIAN PERSPECTIVE ON INCLUSIVE EDUCATION

The Palestinian Territory is a conflict area that has for many years struggled for basic needs due to one of the longest wars in history. Although inclusive education could naturally be seen as last on a long list of priorities, there are, nonetheless, laws and regulations in place related to its adoption and implementation.

From a historical perspective, it is clear that over the last few decades Palestine has come a long way in terms of disability rights, including inclusive education rights. The second part of the special announcement on the rights of people with intellectual disabilities issued in 1971 gave, for example 'some educational rights' to individuals with such disabilities stating that:

[T]he individual with mental disability is entitled to be provided with appropriate health/medical care, some extent of education, training, rehabilitation and guidance. In addition to that, his abilities and capacities should be improved to the maximum possible level.

Then in 1975, the sixth article of the special announcement on the rights of people with intellectual disabilities stated that:

[T]he individual with disability is entitled to medical, psychological and functional treatments including providing artificial body parts and adjustment equipment. S/He also, has the right to be offered social and educational rehabilitation. These programs should assist him develop his abilities in order to secure his employment and facilitate the social integration process.

Later, in 1983, education was seen as part of the National Rehabilitation Program for People With Disabilities. The general conference of the National Labour Organization adopted Agreement No. 159 and Recommendation No. 168 regarding vocational rehabilitation and employment of people with disabilities as part of their efforts to ensure the right of people with disability to be offered training and occupations based on equal chances and opportunities. This agreement also confirmed that it is fundamental for each country that adopts rehabilitation policies for people with disabilities to seek to provide appropriate vocational rehabilitation chances and working opportunities in the free labour market.

Article 10 of Section 4 of the 1994 law of disabled rights in Palestinian stressed the right of education as part of the rights of disabled citizens. The article states the following:

The Ministry of Social Affairs should be responsible for liaising with the concerned parties/agencies to facilitate the education and the rehabilitation of disabled citizens to insure:

- Disabled rights to obtain equal opportunities to enrol in schools and universities within the curriculum offered in such institutes .
- Provision of assessment to define his/her needs according to the nature of the disability.
- Provision of modified curriculum, teaching aids, and materials.
- Provision of education for the disabled according to their needs.
- Provision of human resources and specialists for each disabled person according to his/her disability. (Palestinian Independent Association for Citizens' Rights, 2006, Report 47, p. 74)

A decade later, in 2004, the Palestinian Child Act was released. Section 41 of the Act states that:

1. A child with special needs has the same right as others to be educated in schools and educational institutes
2. In the case of exceptional and profound disability the government should provide alternative placement in special school/centres as long as:

   a. Curriculum and provisions are the same as in the regular school.
   b. The institution is close and easily accessible from where s/he lives.
   c. The institute provides all stages of education.
   d. Provision of human resources needed for their education and rehabilitation.

However, the parliament is yet to undertake responsibility for implementing the aforementioned legislation as it is instructed by article 73 of the same act (Palestinian Independent Association for Citizens' Rights, 2006, Report 47, p. 74).

Looking at some figures and facts on the Palestinian ground, many of the disabled and those with special needs do not get an equal chance for education, and 48.3% of them are, unfortunately, illiterate (Palestinian Independent Association for Citizens' Rights, 2006, Report 47, p. 75). As for inclusion in regular schools and universities, the ratio is quite low, despite claims from officials that the government is doing its best to provide inclusive education under such difficult circumstances and with so few resources. A national statistic in 2004 found that there were only 200 students enrolled in Palestinian national universities (11 in total in the Gaza Strip and the West Bank) out of 130,000 university students all together. In Nables, for example, out of 77,745 learners in government schools in the 2005–2006 academic year, there were only 401 disabled children. This diminutive 5% was in line with a broader national study published following the academic year 2003–2004. The Ministry of Education study revealed that among 706,105 learners in government schools in Palestine there are a mere 3,280 disabled learners.[21]

Table 2.1 represents the education level of 60 disabled persons across the West Bank and Gaza Strip randomly interviewed by the Palestinian Independent Association for Citizens' Rights.

The preceding national statistic and the random small scale research in Palestine shows that, despite what is, in theory, stated by the government in a form or a federal act, in practice the government needs to improve the educational provisions offered for individuals with special needs. A clear example of the deficiency of budget allocated to inclusive education which is published and thus in the public domain can be seen in the 5-year plan, 2000–2004, for the Ministry of Higher Education. The budget allocated in US dollars is 232.6 million, with US$ 222.9 million from that for salaries for the Higher Education Department.[22] It is interesting to note that nothing is allocated to special accommodation or modification to facilitate the inclusion of students with special needs and disabilities.

In an interview, the Head of Planning at the Ministry of Education stressed the commitment to inclusive education in the next 5-year plan, 2007–2011. He stated that:

The plan is to insure that all necessary modifications to facilitate inclusion for the disabled are taken into account so all government schools

*Table 2.1*  Number of Persons with Disabilities and Educational Level in the West Bank and Gaza Strip

| Education Level/Obtained Qualifications | Number of Persons with Disabilities |
| --- | --- |
| Master's (physical disabilities) | 2 |
| Master's (visual impairments) | 1 |
| Bachelor's (physical disabilites) | 6 |
| Bachelor's (visual impairments) | 3 |
| Bachelor's (hearing and communication impairments) | 1 |
| Higher diploma | 5 |
| Secondary school | 10 |
| Middle school | 12 |
| Primary | 6 |
| Illiterate | 14 |
| Total | 60 |

must be accessible including transportation to and from school. Ministry must insure that budget allocated for such facilities as well as the required assistive technologies for all disabilities and special needs is included in the government budget not relying on NGOs to provide for such services. This is to insure maximum inclusion and participation of all learners in government schools.

In the plan there will also be consideration to professional development for teachers to prepare them for inclusion to ensure smooth transition and effective education for all. Accessibility for all schools is to be built into the proposed plan.

On the ground, however, reality differs to a great extent. On the issues of accessibility and schools being inclusive and accessible for all, a Palestinian participant (R.A.) from Janin was interviewed. He had 75% physical impairments and, despite being a victim of lack of suitable accessibility and human resources, he excelled in primary school. He stated:

At the primary level I did not get into many problems and I excelled at all subjects. When I moved to secondary, however I found lots of problems. the school was around 3 kilometers away, and the road was not accessible, in spite of my father's financial situation. We did not have enough money to ride a bus or hire a car. I used to walk in the rain or in the burning sun, despite my disability. I hated schools and I hated studying all together. What made things worse was the stigma . . . the principal used to call me the creep because I had a physical disability . . . especially when he was doing this in front of all other students . . . so I just hated school. (Palestinian Independent Association for citizens' rights, 2006, Report 47, pp. 80–81)

A citizen (H.S.) who has a 50% physical disability stated that:

The school was never ready for me, both building and infrastructure wise. The stairs were high, and the 2nd floor was not designed for cases like me all. Toilets were not modified for people with special needs. The principal was the main barrier to inclusion and to me and my academic achievement. He could not care less about my circumstances and needs, he used to call me names and hit me. (Palestinian Independent Association for Citizens' Rights, 2006, Report 47, p. 81)

A female with physical disabilities from Al Khalil acknowledges the physical barriers but praises the support from peers and those who were working at the school. She stated that:

Studying in primary and secondary was not easy as the schools were not accessible inside or outside of the classrooms. For example, each classroom had about 5 steps to climb in order to get in. However the support of my peers and teachers was amazing . . . they just got me through all the way until I got my certificate and went on to get a diploma afterwards. (Palestinian Independent Association for Citizens' Rights, 2006, Report 47, p. 81)

### 2.8.1 Inclusive Education Program

The Ministry of Higher Education in Palestine adopted the inclusive education philosophy in its schools in 1997, through including students with special needs gradually in government schools. It also started applying experimental projects for 3 years, in 1997, 1998 and 1999, funded by the Swedish and Norwegian Organization "DYA CONIA and NAD" under the name of "Saving the Swedish Child" Organization with technical support by UNESCO.

The targeted category in this project was primary students from Grades 1 to 4. This program aimed to provide education for all students, including students with disabilities, through including them in the school system by improving teachers' skills to be able to deal with them professionally. In addition to that, it worked on preparing schools to develop appropriate substructure to meet the required needs of students with special needs and improve different teaching methodologies.

The estimated number of students with special needs was 3,280 students in 2003/2004, 1,119 students of which are enrolled in the inclusive education program that was provided by the Ministry. They were distributed across 305 schools in 2003/2004, which is considered great progress compared to other government schools in 1997/1998 where there were only 30 schools.

In 2003/2004, the Ministry of Higher Education equipped 523 government school buildings in order to be able to accept students with mild disabilities that were able to learn.

Regarding the framework of this program, many team workers were employed from provinces (two to three teams from each province) to train teachers, enhance the schools' physical environment, facilitate students' inclusion and provide technical support, where each member of the team was responsible for 5 to 10 schools.

There is also a question on the probability of qualifying and equipping all the government schools (1,726 schools), in addition to providing teaching facilities to all students with special needs—taking into consideration their various types of disabilities—in order to facilitate or make possible the acquisition of their education from primary through to the end of secondary level. However, qualifying schools not only includes fixing schools' substations, but also providing teaching aids and equipment to assist the special needs students, such as medical hearing aids, Braille machines, teaching sign language, special laboratories and recording lectures.

A citizen (M.S.) from Ramal-lah and Beira Province who is visually impaired explained the effect of the lack of learning equipment in schools on his future vocational and academic career. He stated that:

> I needed printed materials in Braille code and they was not provided for me at the Secondary and University level, therefore, I depended on my listening in the lectures which helped me pass through the secondary level. However, I failed to overcome these obstacles at the university level and, in addition to that, many other types of equipment- such as, recorded tapes, interactive computers and a tape recorder- were very essential for me, but were not available and this affected my studies. (Palestinian Independent Association for Citizens' Rights, 2006, Report 47, pp. 80–81)

He added,

> [E]ven the teachers in the high school were not qualified to teach special needs students, and as a result of the society's view about people with disabilities and of the Ministry's negligence towards me, I failed in the subject English in the first semester of the twelfth grade. However, in the second semester, I printed the textbook, studied it, and passed the exams. Furthermore, the Ministry didn't provide me with Braille machines, which led me to borrow it from other places. Another obstacle was my stick: I was not provided with one in the school, so I had to buy it myself. Because the school didn't provide me with printed books in Braille, I had to print all the school and University's textbooks by myself to be able to study them, yet I paid all the school's fees just like regular students. However, I was granted some discounts in university fees after struggling every semester with the university's accountants and administration. (Palestinian Independent Association for Citizens' Rights, 2006, Report 47, p. 92)

According to Report 47 by the Palestinian Independent Association for Citizens' Rights (2006), the total number of educational institutes in the West Bank and Gaza that provided education for students with hearing disabilities during 2005/2006 was 17 schools, in which 1,310 students with hearing disabilities were enrolled. This means that they represented 55% of the total number of students with hearing disabilities (2,368) between 1 and 19 years old. This figure indicates that there are 1,058 students with hearing disabilities who are not officially enrolled in primary schools. On the other hand, there are only two education institutes that provide education to students with hearing disabilities up to Grade 11: Our Children with Hearing Disabilities Institute in Gaza and the Integral Communication Institute in the West Bank. Most other schools provide education for them up to the sixth and seventh grades. As a result, students with hearing disabilities are deprived of secondary and university education, which means that all the resources that are invested in their education are wasted. This issue explains the low number of students with different special needs enrolled in universities, and it proves that the educational efforts provided for students with special needs are below the expected level and are not sufficient to reach the desired goals.

Y.S. is a 17-year-old student from Jenin Province with hearing and communication disabilities. He finished his primary education until Grade 7 at Al-Hana school for students with hearing and communication disabilities, but he could not go any further because there were no specialized schools for higher grades (elementary and secondary) education. Furthermore, the coordinator of the Committee for Improvement of Services for Students with Hearing Disability in Jenin was asked about the reality of the education of students with hearing and communication disabilities, and he commented:

> [I]ndividuals with hearing and communication disabilities in Jenin attend Al-Hana school until grade seven and after that, they either have to return to their homes or continue doing other external activities with the school. Only a few of them attend the vocational training because of the lack of professional and qualified teaching staff in the vocational institutes which, in return, makes it difficult for those students to continue.

Palestinian Independent Association for Citizens' Rights Report 47 (2006) confirms that

> [O]nly three of the students with special needs who finished their studies in Al-Hana School joined another secondary school and had their final exams, but none of them passed last year again due to a lack of qualified teaching staff in the Ministry of Education and because they were not allowed to be provided with translators from outside the education staff, although the Ministry's policy in this field allows translators to be provided for students with special needs in all areas. For example, Jordan is applying this policy and it provides translators in the exam halls. (p. 103)

The Ministry of Higher Education in Palestine has always adopted the principle that "education is the right of everyone." Hence, it established a Special Education Department in 1996 to be responsible for applying the polices that are related to helping people with disabilities to obtain their right in education; to plan and coordinate with related institutions to contribute to achieve the goal of education for everyone. The Ministry also worked on the framework strategy "learning does not exclude anyone." In an interview with a top official at the Ministry of Education, he commented on the issue of inclusive education as a right for all, stating:

It is the right of every Palestinian child to be educated and this does not exclude any student, regardless of individual differences or any other difficulties. It also considers and meets their individual needs through preparing government schools to admit special needs children in order to integrate them with their peers and provide the required environment to help them.

In realty though, even at a higher level of education, the Palestinian government did not set up any regulations to reduce the educational expenses for students with special needs in terms of educational equipment and university fees. The government did not specify any budget that covers educational expenses for students with special needs; instead they remained dependent on contributions from different organizations in the society and on individual donations. Therefore, students with special needs are not exempt from any educational fees from universities in Palestine nor are they getting a fair chance when external help is available. In 2005, the Ministry of Higher Education in Palestine supervised scholarships donated by Saudi Arabia for many universities in Palestine. Ironically, these scholarships were granted to orphans and financially deprived students, but not to any student with special needs or disabilities. This simply indicates lack of support to improve the right of education for individuals with disabilities in Palestine.

M.G. from Ramal-lah and Al-Bira Province confirmed this status. He has 65% health impairments and commented on the provision of university education for individuals with disabilities in Palestine, stating, "I finished my secondary education successfully but was not able to join any university because of my financial situation; hence I neither continued university nor asked for any assistance" (Palestinian Independent Association for Citizens' Rights, 2006, Report 47, p. 53).

In general, we can say most of the services that are provided by different countries and international organizations are considered part of the 'Rehabilitation Right.' Even the public awareness program for special needs rights is considered as 'community rehabilitation.' If one wishes to look at the issue of education versus the tendency to opt for vocational education, we find that although education is now seen as an important issue for citizens with special needs and disabilities, there are strong beliefs and attitudes towards the idea of vocational education as the best option for people with disability among Palestinians.

The government in Palestine issued many regulations on the right of vocational rehabilitation for people with disabilities in more details compared to other rights that are related to people with disabilities. For example, the fifth regulation on the right of people with disabilities states:

[T]he government should provide different kinds of vocational rehabilitation for people with disabilities according to the type of disability, and they should contribute with no more that 25% of the total cost.

However, due to the occupation conditions [war], people with disabilities are exempted from paying that contribution.

On the other hand, Regulation No. 10 stated that:

[T]he Ministry of Social Affairs is responsible for coordinating with concerned authorities to work on the rehabilitation and employment of people with disabilities through preparing professional and qualified staff to work with different categories of special needs.

The Rehabilitation Services Program also ensures the right of people with disabilities' enrolment in vocational training institutes and rehabilitation services based on the 'equal chances for people with disabilities' principle. All government and non-government organizations were required to accept not less than 5% of people with disability to work in their firms with regards to their conditions and to prepare the working environment to be suitable for them. In addition to that, private sectors were encouraged to employ people with disabilities through a deduction of a percentage of their salaries from the income tax of those companies.

The executive regulation of the Special Needs Rights No. 12 had further details with regard to organizing vocational trainings for them. It stated that:

[T]he Ministry of Social Affairs should coordinate with related associations to provide the required care and rehabilitation for people with disabilities in the working fields:

1. All government and non-government sectors are required to employ not less than 5% of people with disability with suitable jobs in their organizations.
2. The Ministry and the concerned authorities are required to provide jobs for trained special needs and keep up-to-date statistics of those who joined the vocational training.
3. The Ministry of Labour has to improve purposeful vocational training for people of disability to enable them to work according to their needs.
4. The Ministry of Social Affairs should encourage the local community and employers to provide jobs for people with disabilities. Hence, this will result in overcoming the fear of not knowing how deal with them; the fear of having low production due to their incompetence and slowness; and the fear of covering the expense of emergency accidents, absence and sick leaves. Those fears could be worked on through conducting awareness among employers, people with disabilities and their families of the importance of special needs people's employment and to reduce the level of the fear of employing them.

The fifth article from the same regulation is related to protected jobs to rehabilitate people with disabilities. It stated that:

1. [T]he Ministry of Social Affairs will issue licenses to establish special institutes and centres to rehabilitate and employ people with disabilities under the Protected Works regulation.
2. The Ministry of Social Affairs should monitor and observe the work of those centres to provide the best services based on special education concepts and the concept of protecting people with disabilities from being misused.
3. The Ministry will provide all the required financial, emotional support and rehabilitation services to the centres that need daytime care.
4. The centres will employ people with severe disabilities that cannot be employed in the local working market.

Internationally, the third rule of the unified regulation in 1993 on achieving equal chances for people with disabilities stated that:

[C]ountries should provide rehabilitation services for its people with disability in order to be able to reach to their highest level of independence and performance as well as maintaining them. Furthermore, they should prepare local rehabilitation programs for all different categories of people with disabilities. These programs should be based on their actual needs, full participation and equality concepts. They should include different types of activities such as basic training that aims to improve their performance; advice to the people with disability and their families; programs that deal with building their self-esteem and other assessments' services. The rehabilitation programs should be offered to all types of people with disabilities, including the mildly and severely disabled.

On the ground, however, the picture differs dramatically. The vocational rehabilitation services are distributed to private and government sectors in Palestine. These services also are provided to national foreign organizations, national aid agencies and the semi-government sectors. However, in general, the private sectors provide the highest services in rehabilitation programs compare to the government sectors which provide 10% of these services. As a result, the North Bank of West Thafa and many other provinces in the country lack numerous governmental vocational rehabilitation centres.

This shortage has lead to the deprivation for many people with disabilities of essential rehabilitation services as these people are often unable to access regularly the services due to transportation difficulties and limited resources. On the national level also, there is an absence of general policies in the rehabilitation field and shortage of effective strategies to coordinate between the private and public sectors in areas that lack vocational rehabilitation centres.

The local citizen (R.A.) from Jenin commented that "because of the lack of vocational rehabilitation centres in Jenin and due to my financial situation, I was not able to join other rehabilitation centres in Nables and RamAl-lah. As a result, I was deprived of those services."

Table 2.2 describes the institutions that offer services to people with disabilities in the West Bank provinces.[23]

It is noticed from the statements of interviewed people with disabilities that a minority of them received vocational rehabilitation, and often those rehabilitation programs were provided only for people with physical disabilities rather than different types of disabilities.

*Table 2.2*  Institutions that Offer Services to People with Disabilities in the West Bank Provinces

| Type of Disability | Total | Defense & Support | Moving | Mental | Speaking | Seeing | Hearing |
|---|---|---|---|---|---|---|---|
| City | | | | | | | |
| Jerusalem | 13 | | 4 | 2 | 3 | 4 | |
| Ramallah | 18 | 3 | 7 | 2 | 2 | 1 | 3 |
| Bethlehem | 21 | | 7 | 7 | 2 | 3 | 2 |
| Hebron | 17 | 2 | 7 | 2 | 3 | 1 | 2 |
| Jericho | 1 | | 1 | | | | |
| Nablus | 16 | 2 | 6 | 3 | 3 | 2 | |
| Tulkarem | 11 | 2 | 1 | 3 | 2 | | 3 |
| Jenin | 8 | 1 | 4 | | 1 | 1 | 1 |
| Deir Al Balah | 4 | | 2 | | | | 2 |
| North Gaza | 8 | 1 | | 6 | | | 1 |
| Gaza | 22 | 2 | 9 | 1 | 3 | 4 | 3 |
| Rafah | 4 | 1 | | 1 | 2 | | |
| Total | 143 | 14 | 48 | 27 | 21 | 16 | 17 |

*Note*: From Palestinian Independent Association for Citizens' Rights (2006), Report 47. Translated from the Arabic.

Furthermore, most of the vocational rehabilitation services were provided by private charity organizations, such as the Christian Youth Committee and other specialized organizations in this field, and some government organizations that specialized in training people with disabilities, most of which complain about lack of organizations in the vocational rehabilitation field.

While lack of resources due to difficulties accessing education and severe financial strain on the government prevent many learners from getting into schools in general, and in inclusive settings in particular, some non-profit charities stepped in to help. The Christian Youth Committee in Palestine is one of the organizations involved in special needs fields. It aims to train, rehabilitate and guide people with disabilities psychologically, physically and socially in the West Bank of Thabfa. It also has many branches in many different provinces. In an interview, the assistant director of the organisation commented that "the rehabilitation program of this organization for people with physical disabilities, considered one of the biggest active programs in the West Bank of Thabfa, provides professional mentors and site staff."

It is clear that the Palestinian society developed a series of laws to ensure the educational rights for people with special needs and disabilities. There are laws and legislations to support and promote inclusive education and encourage schools to be accessible in Palestine. However, there are a number of issues that act as barriers to the implementation of such laws in Palestinian society. Currently there is a classic scenario of policy makers in a 'catching up with the rest of the world' mood, but plenty needs to be done culturally and internally to ensure that this is what the majority wants. Research in the area of inclusive education is minimal so it is hardly known to what extent it is accepted as a practice in the Palestinian Territory. If there are any publications they mainly focus on inclusion of individuals with physical disabilities with no mention of other disabilities. There is a desperate need for training for school staff and especially administrative and management staff as was revealed in interviews of participants. Funding for the implementation of the policy is impossible in a place where daily essentials are a struggle for the majority of people.

Accessibility and transpiration were, and still will be, the main reason for limiting the process of special needs students' enrolment in government schools and universities, and also has the direct impact of depriving many people with disabilities from getting their basic school and university education. When the individual with disability cannot move comfortably in his/her school, or when his/her required needs with regards to his/her disability are not met, or when there are no professional and trained teaching staff available, then, definitely, the individual with disability will have to face the reality of not having the chance to learn in schools even if it was allowed by law.

As for financial resources, in theory it has been taken care of. Article 10 of Section 4 of the 1994 law of disabled rights in Palestinian states, "Students with special needs should be exempted or be offered deduction from educational fees or reduced fees in schools and universities" (Article 10, Section 4, 1994 law of disabled rights in Palestine). This statement is considered a fundamental insurance that the government could provide special needs families to encourage sending their children to schools instead of stopping them because of the high schools fees. However, school fees are not an obstacle in Palestine, because most schools provide free education for all children, including children with special needs, from primary until secondary level. But the most important issue is providing free educational assistance for students with special needs, not just waiving the fees. It is good that they are to be provided with primary and secondary education, but to be educated effectively they should be assisted to further their education through either university or alternative educational options. The reason for that is because university fees are considerably higher compared to primary educational fees.

Community is a socially constructed entity (Vygotsky, 1978) composed of a collective of individuals in the same place at the same time. Struggle within that entity, whether over resources, power, status, gender or something else (finite but inherently valuable), creates a basis for conflict. Thus, the dynamic nature of a school community is one in which its members actively construct and reconstruct their knowledge with each other through their contested interactions about education (Barnett & Fallon, 2007, p. 2).

To conclude, the conflict between Israel and Palestine is a long-standing conflict situation that is difficult to resolve due to several factors which it is not the intention of this book to explore. In a region of conflict that is full of hate and aggression, where the Israeli government claims that the security of its people is a prime priority and makes every effort to ensure that, while Palestinian suicide bombers, in a desperate attempt to protest, essentially become human bombs (Schweitzer, 2001), all activities are overshadowed by war. On the other hand, and since the Six Day War, the Israeli community has attracted some of the most militant groups among the settlers in the West Bank and other Palestinian territories, responsible for severe violence against Palestinians, including harassment, car bombs and attempts to blow up the Dome of the Rock mosque itself (Røislien, 2007, p. 170). In such difficult circumstances we find that inclusive education is simply overlooked in the Palestinian society as the basic needs are not met due to poverty and financial strains. There are no doubts that there are various attempts to acknowledge the educational rights of people with disabilities and special needs as stated by Report 47 of the Palestinian Independent Association for Citizens' Rights (2006): "[T]he right for education should be granted to all disabled citizens in order to enable them to be productive and to fulfil their potential to serve their community" (p. 72). It can be strongly argued, however, that inclusive education is virtually not a priority, and disability issues in general are last on the list in one of the most notorious war zones on earth.

## 2.9  DISCUSSION

This chapter looked at the six GCC countries as well as three Middle Eastern countries reviewed in this book. It began with an examination of inclusive education in the Kingdom of Saudi Arabia. It explored, sensitively though, the current status on inclusive education. It also looks at the position of the largest GCC country on adoption and ratification of the 2004 UN Convention on the Rights of Persons With Disabilities, including access to regular mainstream education. However, the current situation seems rather vague within a country that is committed to inclusion, but other issues distract the attention of decision- makers, like fighting terrorism and ensuring that nothing gets in the way of the development of the country. The chapter then explored the famous, better-known, leading Kuwaiti experience with inclusion. It explored the current provision on offer and the effect on the lives of Kuwaiti learners with special needs in a country that was the first to adopt any form of inclusive strategy in the Gulf area, but to a degree opted for a category-based education system and stuck to it. Qatar's scattered, but well-planned pilot inclusive experience was then examined in light of the latest, yet controversial educational reform with more independent schools that are run as private institutions with allocated funds from the government. With the help of a very dedicated disability high profile royalty (HRH Sheika Hesa Al-Thani), the country indeed leaped ahead in providing services for learners with disabilities.

The chapter then moved to the Omani inclusive practice, especially in rural areas and the geographical challenges that act as obstacles on the way of any attempt to implementing inclusion. Bahrain, a small GCC country but with a big inclusion agenda, was then discussed. Inclusive education in the United Arab Emirates (UAE), the last GCC country and the most fast-developing and dynamic, was not discussed in this chapter as it will be dealt with in details in the following chapter as an example of how a country is going from exclusion to inclusion and all the related cultural, political and certainly practical contexts.

Moving to three examples from the Middle East, carefully selected for various purposes as stated in the introductory chapter, Egypt was a natural target for its population and political status among the Arabs. The slow-moving inclusion process with many voices that call for taking the pilot project to a larger level nationwide, in times where many Egyptians are struggling with daily needs, was explored. Tunisia, the first African-Arab country to ratify the UN convention on Rights of Persons With Disabilities and commit to the international law related to inclusive policy was presented in this chapter. Finally, the chapter ended with the rather interesting experience of the Palestinian Territory. Inclusion in the war zone that represents a Palestinian perspective on inclusive education concludes this cross-cultural chapter. The purpose of this brief discussion is not by any means to elect what is better and what is worse in dealing with inclusion in different settings, nor to illustrate what is similar or what is different, but most of all what could be learnt from each other in the quest for inclusion: This discussion will be the focus of the final chapter.

# 3 Inclusion in the UAE
## Theory, Culture and Practice

### 3.1 UAE BACKGROUND

Located on the coast of the Arabian Gulf, the United Arab Emirates (UAE) is a wealthy newly-formed nation. The country was established in 1971 and it consists of seven emirates. The oil revenues and the open economy with a high per capita income surely generate great wealth for its citizens (CIA, 2007).

Despite being a young country, the UAE has made significant progress in different areas while moving from being a sheikhdom desert nation to a modern country benefiting from the discovery of oil which is the major source of income. Gaad, et al. (2006) states that the advancement of the county is the result of oil and gas, together with the recent upsurge of tourism, which has made the nation into an ultra modern state of the world. Accordingly, a significant change has occurred in all sectors in the UAE including economy, social development, health and, naturally, education (p. 134).

The Emiratis (UAE nationals) comprise about 20% of the total population. Besides the Emiratis, there are various nationalities referred to as 'expatriates' or 'expats' for short, such as those from other Arab countries, Iranians, Filipinos, Indians, and large numbers of Europeans and Americans.

Education is compulsory until Grade 9 and free for all UAE nationals. Non-nationals attend private schools which cater to the diversity in their needs and languages. The philosophy behind education in the UAE is based on the Islamic human rights which are universal human rights as well. These are:

• The right to equality.
• The right to social welfare and the basic necessities of life.
• The right to dignity and not to be abused or ridiculed.
• The right of education (Bradshaw, Tennant, & Lydiatt, 2004, p. 50).

The educational system in the UAE is comprised of public and private sectors. The Ministry of Education (MOE) in the UAE is in charge of both sectors in all emirates. Nevertheless, the responsibility that the ministry plays in the public sector is much broader than its responsibility in the private one (Bradshaw et al., 2004). The public sector is funded and controlled by the federal government—that is, the MOE—that provides free education exclusively to the citizens of this country. Just recently, it was permitted for expatriates from Arabic nations to apply for placement in MOE schools but with a paid annual school fee. MOE schools are based on and influenced strongly by Arabic and Islamic values. The medium of instruction is Arabic, apart from a second language, English, which is taught from Grade 1 at the primary level and onwards. Apart from the kindergarten level and with the exception of remote rural areas, learners at all other school stages are of a single gender.

The MOE schools are divided into four stages as follows: The kindergarten stage admits learners of 4 to 5 years. The primary stage, which lasts 6 years, admits learners between 6 and 12 years old and is compulsory for all UAE nationals. The intermediate level lasts 3 years and learners of 12 to 15 are enrolled in such classes. The secondary level lasts 3 years and it caters to learners aged 15 to 18 years old. All learners at the end of the third secondary year, after passing a general school board exam, are awarded with secondary school certificates. There are technical schools, however, and they start from Year 6 onwards and enrol learners from 12 to 18 years of age. A technical secondary diploma is then awarded to a student after he/she successfully passes the final examination.

As far as the private sector is concerned, a large number of schools have sprung up along with the booming economy due to the huge expatriate population community residing in the UAE. In order to educate their citizens and satisfy their cultural and religious needs, many nationalities have opened schools. These schools are licensed and supervised by the MOE. As was stated by Gaad et al. (2006), "[T]he private sector is growing faster than the public sector as many new schools have come up" (p. 293). Syllabus and curriculum may vary according to the nationality they cater to, however the division of the various school stages is nearly the same.

## 3.2   EDUCATING INDIVIDUALS WITH SPECIAL NEEDS IN THE UAE

In due course, it became apparent that there were not enough UAE national teachers to cover all public schools and subjects for a sustained period of time; therefore the country's government hired teachers from other countries to staff the schools (Rugh, 1997). Development in the field of education has been undertaken since the initiation of the formal education system, and the country has catered to learners in general education; however, a new need has arisen to cater to learners with special needs in the education system.

The provision for learners with special needs varies, but it can be divided into public and private sectors in the mainstream schools, as well as segregated special needs centres previously known as 'disabled welfare and rehabilitation centres' where the majority of such learners are served. Later on, such centres changed their names to 'centres for people with special needs' due to pressure from some advocacy groups. Whereas the regular schools are either controlled or supervised by MOE, the special needs centres, both government and private, come under the Ministry of Social Affairs.

The MOE is committed to providing help and support to youngsters with special needs who have difficulty coping with mainstream classes. Many public schools offer specialised aid in two ways. There are resource rooms and special needs classes. The resource room is based on a pull-out system that deals with learners who have difficulties in a particular subject, especially Arabic/maths. Special sessions are given to those who need extra help. According to Bradshaw et al. (2004), "The resources room program provides intensive small group remedial instructional services in a pull out system. Grouping varies from four to five learners" (p. 52).

As far as special classes were concerned, before the new federal law (see later discussion for more details), public schools accepted learners with an IQ of 75 and those with mild disabilities. However, things changed after the issuance of the law: Public schools have started to accept, among others, learners with moderate hearing difficulties and visual impairments. Moreover, learners such as those with Down syndrome, regardless of their cognitive ability, who Gaad (2001) referred to as natural candidates for special needs centres, were enrolled on trial bases in four public schools.

The MOE started catering to learners with special needs by the year 1980, when the first five special education classes were opened for 40 learners in different elementary schools in the UAE (Abood, 2005). Special classes are full-time services for a group of learners with special needs. Identification of those who have special needs may vary internationally, but for MOE schools it signified those who are referred by their first grade teachers after 6 months in schooling as 'not coping with regular education' and/or those who are referred from either of the two ministries involved: the Ministry of Health (MOH) and the Ministry of Social Affairs (MOSA). These classes are allocated in the mainstream school with a small number of learners who are taught by a teacher with a special needs background. Those classes ranged from Grade 1 to 3 at the basic level of education. By 1985, the special classes were expanded to cover more schools. Slow learners and under achieving learners (as they are known in the UAE contexts) were included, whereas learners with intellectual disabilities were excluded and sent to centres of special needs under the authority of the MOSA. The reason for transferring them there was usually due to their low IQ (below 70) and because they were making insufficient progress in the schools. Learners who could not progress academically to meet the outcome of their grade levels were shifted to special education evening classes (Abood, 2005) and those below IQ 70 were shifted to centres of special needs.

In 1990, resource rooms were opened in the elementary schools in the country. Resource rooms are a part-time service for several groups of learners who join those rooms during their school day, twice or three times a week according to their needs. Each group consists of 10 to 12 learners. Teachers of those rooms are qualified teachers with a background in special needs. Furthermore, in 2000 a new service was added to the special needs provision: speech and language therapy. Additionally, learners with sensory disabilities could enrol in schools, but without support. Both the special classes and the resource rooms in the schools were regulated by the MOE and followed the department of special needs in the Ministry. This department was known as the Department of Special Abilities.

It is interesting to note that the MOE's schools used to accept certain and less obvious categories of special needs. An example of this is that learners with learning difficulties were enrolled easily in schools as it is not an immediately discernible disability. Other obvious categories of special needs, such as learners with Down syndrome or those with physical impairment, were not accepted at schools and were sent to the centres of special needs where they might not even be enrolled if their IQ was above 70 as these centres accepted only learners with an IQ below 70.

Currently, learners with specific non visible/physical special needs (ADHD or dyslexia, for example) enter free government schools if they are UAE nationals, whereas non-nationals enrol their learners with special needs either in private schools, if possible, or in private special needs centres. Other learners with obvious special needs, like Down syndrome, are enrolled in special needs centres. As mentioned earlier, those government centres are therapy and rehabilitation focused and are open for UAE nationals and private centres which charge fees are open for other nationalities.

## 3.3 INCLUSIVE EDUCATION AND THE FEDERAL LAW 29/2006

For an educational system to support and enforce inclusion in institutions, it needs to have the backing of legislation. As Colebatch (2000) states, "[P]olicy is what government decides to do" (p. 61), and that support of the legislation was achieved when the first law for special needs was passed in 2006. However, it can be argued that there are many matters that still need to evolve legally. Policy-wise, certain hurdles have yet to be overcome before the vision of all learners receiving a fair education materializes. One of the major issues, which is currently hindering the process of inclusive education for all learners in the UAE, is that it is under two ministries—the MOE and the MOSA—and, until recently it was even under a third ministry—the MOH. According to Gaad (2004b) this dual management is not only questioned from a human rights perspective, but also questions have been raised about its efficiency. It was argued all along that having two separate policies does not help social or educational inclusion of learners with special needs, for that in turn will affect their job prospects and thus hinder total inclusion into the society. This is a clear obstacle in achieving the goals of providing equal rights and opportunity.

Inclusion of learners with special needs in mainstream schools is an international phenomenon that is making its way to the UAE. Keeping in line with the trend of 'education for all', and reaffirming the pledge in the Salamanca Statement, the world leaders declared that they would make sure of the protection of the right of education of every child, without any discrimination and that includes disability (UNESCO, 1994). The UAE was rather slow in responding to this declaration and later issued the Federal Law No. 29/2006), on the rights of people with disabilities, including those with special needs, to be educated (Farouk, 2008). The inclusion approach was recently adopted on a pilot basis following pressure from parental and advocacy groups to implement the law. The law includes education for learners with special needs in the least restrictive environment as a fundamental right. The declaration of the law was in March 2006 but it is far from being fully adopted.

Prior to the declaration of this law, educating learners with special needs was the responsibility of three ministries: the MOH, the MOSA and the MOE. The MOH used to provide informal education for learners who stay permanently in hospitals for one reason or another, such as being terminally ill or being abandoned. Additionally, some education was provided to learners who were regular visitors to the physiotherapy department. Those services are no longer in existence. Additionally, the MOSA used to provide education for learners with special needs in a segregated setting outside the mainstream school. They still exist, but are changing in function as the move towards catering to special needs in schools is implemented under the authority of the MOE. Those centres used to adopt mostly a welfare model with less education. Usually their services were in either speech therapy or physiotherapy with less education.

The all new federal law for the rights of persons with special needs was declared after being long anticipated by many stakeholders, parents and disability advocates. The law in general aims at protecting the rights of the person with special needs by providing them with appropriate services in three main areas: education, health and employment. In the education field, the law guarantees access to equal opportunities to education with all educational organizations for learners with special needs. Therefore, the MOE started piloting projects which include some learners with special needs in mainstream classes. Article 2 of the law presented the aim of adopting such a law stating:

This law aims at protecting the rights of the person with special needs and providing him with all needed services appropriate to his capacities and abilities. His special needs shall not be a reason to prevent the person with special needs from obtaining the said rights and services, especially those related to the special care, social, economical, health, educational, professional, cultural and entertaining services. (UAE Federal Law No. 29/2006, Article 2)

Education was one of several rights given to persons with special needs. The law did not insist that schools be the only place for providing education to learners with special needs. On the contrary, it has given many options for providing education to learners with special needs. Article 9 stated in general the role of special centres for learners with special needs. Additionally, Articles 12, 13, 14 and 15 are concerned with education of those learners. In order to get a full idea about the background of implementing inclusion in education as a pilot project in the UAE, a brief summary of the law is presented.

Article 9 stated that: "The Ministry shall establish, in collaboration with the competent authority centres, organizations, and institutes specialized in the care, training and rehabilitation of persons with special needs." The law stressed that such centres, organizations and institutes shall hold a responsibility to provide special education for persons with special needs (Article 9:b).

Article 12 stated:

The State guarantees to the person with special needs access to equal opportunities of education within all educational institutions, professional preparation institutions, adult education, and continuous education, whether in normal or private classes when necessary.

In addition, Articles 13, 14 and 15 emphasized education as a fundamental right for persons with special needs. As a response to this federal law, the MOE of the UAE created a plan whereby educational services for learners with special needs were piloted: that is, the MOE plan for implementing inclusion and enhancing special needs services.

Furthermore, Article 15 states:

Pursuant to a resolution by the Council of Ministers, a committee shall be established under the name "Specialized Committee on Education of Persons with Special Needs", . . . and the Minister of Education shall issue a work system for the Committee and its meetings.

The same article outlines the responsibilities of this committee in regards to the education of learners with special needs.

In a public speech, Al Roumi, Minister of Social Affairs (2006), stated that the law that was issued to protect the rights of the special needs has observed all the provisions of the international convention on protecting the rights of this category, slotted for implementation in 2008, in order to involve people with special needs in the development plan adopted by the country.

However, one of the main concerns of stakeholders who have long awaited the law is that there is no clear procedure for the implementation process. As Al Yousef, the director of Takamul,[1] states, a study is currently being carried out to enforce the gradual integration process. Until procedures are worked out, the issue of learners with special needs facing the bureaucracy to be included in a mainstream school will still be there.

There have been many calls by advocates to ratify the UN Convention on the Rights of Persons With Disabilities and to change the current law (29/2006) to be specified for people with disabilities not with special needs. The call for changing the name and the terminology of the law was mainly because of the vagueness of the term 'special needs' in a rather young nation. People with disabilities wanted the law to protect their rights and they felt that having a law dedicated to the larger population with special needs is hindering the implantation of the law and threatening resources allocated for such implementation. In response to advocates and in appreciation of people with disabilities as valued members of society, HH Sheikh khalifa Bin Zayed Al Nahyan, the president of the UAE, issued the historic legislation to urge the Minster of Social Affairs to ratify the UN Convention on the Rights of Persons With Disabilities and to change the name of the current law (29/2006) to be specified for people with 'disabilities' not with 'special needs.'

On 26/12/09, Abu Dhabi: President His Highness Shaikh Khalifa Bin Zayed Al Nahyan has issued a law ratifying the Convention on the Rights of Persons with Disabilities. Federal Law No 116/2009, to be published in the official gazette, instructs the Social Affairs Minister to take the necessary steps for its implementation. Shaikh Khalifa also issued Federal Law No 14/2009 amending Law No 29/2006 on people with special needs. (WAM, UAE News Agency, 26 December 2009. UAE ratified the convention 19th March 2010)

Countries that ratify the convention must take further steps in implementing the guiding principles of the convention in action, and allow for monitoring by the relevant UN committee. There are, as follows, eight guiding principles that underlie the Convention and each one of its specific articles:

a. Respect for inherent dignity, individual autonomy—including the freedom to make one's own choices—and independence of persons
b. Non-discrimination
c. Full and effective participation and inclusion in society
d. Respect for difference and acceptance of persons with disabilities as part of human diversity and humanity

e. Equality of opportunity
f. Accessibility
g. Equality between men and women
h. Respect for the evolving capacities of children with disabilities and respect for the right of children with disabilities to preserve their identities (http://www.un.org/disabilities/default.asp?navid=15&pid=156 accessed Dec/09)

Monitoring of the implementation of the Convention will be followed. Article 33 explains that states must set up national focal points within governments in order to monitor implementation of the Convention's precepts. States must also set up some sort of independent monitoring mechanisms— which usually takes the form of an independent national human rights institution. The full participation of civil society, in particular persons with disabilities and their representative organizations, is essential in the national monitoring and implementation process. International monitoring is achieved via the Committee on the Rights of Persons With Disabilities and the Conference of States Parties (http://www.un.org/disabilities/default.asp?navid=17&pid=157 accessed Dec/09).

## 3.4 CULTURAL ATTITUDES TOWARDS INCLUDING LEARNERS WITH SPECIAL NEEDS IN REGULAR SCHOOLS IN THE UAE

Attitudes drive our behaviour. As individuals and as groups, what we believe and how we feel about a matter largely determines what we do with respect to it. Our behaviour further reinforces our beliefs and feelings (Vash, 2001). Gaad (2004) warned that the attitude of a given community towards people with disabilities will affect the kind of provision made for such individuals. Attitudes towards inclusion are affected by cultural beliefs and values. Therefore, it is important to analyse current cultural beliefs and values if we are to examine the extent to which including learners with special needs in the mainstream is currently accepted, criticized, rejected or applied.

In a society that is growing by the minute and considered as one of the richest and fastest developing countries in the world, learners with special needs face real cultural attitude issues. Alongside the Emiratis' desperation to secure jobs for their minority citizens backed by the nation-wide Emiratisation campaign and the expatriates' desperation to secure and maintain their jobs and tax-free salaries, individuals with special needs can face a real challenge to be heard and granted the provisions they need to reach their full potential and to play a productive part in society. Nonetheless, the picture is not always that gloomy and it does not mean that this society is a ruthless one. In fact, the limited research that was undertaken in the country showed it as a caring society (Gaad, 2001). For the purpose of this chapter, a series of school observations took place where included learners with special needs were observed. The author observed how learners in one classroom helped a classmate with intellectual disability, allowing more time for him to express his views and communicate. In addition, some interviewed participants for another research project (special education supervisors) have indicated that it is common to see some headmasters allowing entry to some severely disabled learners to their schools if they feel sympathy for such learners (Ibrahim, 2008).

It is difficult to understand cultural practice when it comes to systems of referral and assessments, especially in the private sector as the majority of private schools act as business corporations. Schools are meant to nurture morale and self-respect to all learners before delivering appropriate education. Unfortunately, this can be misleading as, in reality, many private schools ignore the needs of learners with special needs, since most private schools are profit-making. A child with special needs requires extra effort, resources and responsibilities, and may weaken the end results (the league tables) that are usually published on the internet for new expatriate parents to browse before considering schooling their learners. Therefore, whereas the society on the whole may be a caring one (Gaad, 2001), the dreaded truth is that at the end of the day learners with special needs are last on the list to be considered in the private sector which forms the biggest chunk of school places.

Gaad (2004c) believes that it is almost impossible not to associate provisions offered for special needs learners without considering the society's traditions and attitudes. Although labelling people with intellectual disabilities has started to change (Gaad, 2004c), one cannot ignore the reality that till now some people still label people with intellectual disabilities as 'idiots' or label those with Down syndrome as 'Mongols.' Attitudes of individuals are indeed influenced by cultural convictions and principles (Gaad, 1998, as cited in Gaad, 2004).

### 3.5 TEACHERS AND INCLUSION: ANXIETY AND ATTITUDES

Teachers in the UAE come from various backgrounds, cultures and religions. Their attitudes towards inclusive education varies, but certain factors such as support and training are important to all to better serve the learners with special needs. The attitudes of teachers are also worth investigating in the UAE because of its effect on the success of inclusion. International research has shown that teachers do not favour the inclusion of learners with special needs in the general classroom (Kavale & Forness, 2000, in Boling, 2007, p. 219). Alghazo and Gaad (2004) and Gaad and Khan (2007) studied the perceptions of teachers in the UAE towards inclusion and found a preference for traditional special education service delivery over full inclusion practices. The teachers bear the heaviest part of catering to the needs of the learners and therefore their acceptance of the principle of inclusion and their willingness to achieve it are paramount. In some cases, the principal of the school is in favour of inclusion, and acts upon it by admitting learners with special needs, but does not share his/her vision with the teachers. On the surface, some learners may have the label 'included,' but they are implicitly excluded from the class activities. Equally, the class size in some UAE schools can be quite big, and incurring extra work because of the presence of learners with special needs, with no incentive, support or training, can take its toll on the teachers. In a research interview, one interviewed teacher spoke about her experience with an included student with autism:

> You can't just take this child and throw him on us. I have to think of every student in the class but he keeps interrupting the work. I really want to help but it is simply not working. My knowledge about autism is limited and his needs are great.

When the attitudes of teachers were researched in the UAE, results were mixed. Alghazo and Gaad (2004) have found that female teachers had more positive attitudes towards inclusion, whereas male teachers had more negative ones. But those mixed attitudes may be attributed to several factors.

## 3.6   PARENTS AND THE QUEST FOR INCLUSION

The child with special needs has the right to be seen and treated as a unique human being with a set of strengths and weaknesses. In many circumstances, people tend to see the disability/condition of the child and fail to consider the child behind that façade. The terminology used to describe people with special needs can constitute a problem if it emphasizes the disability and ignores the person. In this regard, the media can play a crucial role in educating and raising awareness about the correct terminology to use when describing people with special needs. In the UAE, more sensitivity to terminology is shown on the part of the media, and media staff are being trained by some advocacy agencies and NGOs to use the proper terminology. More awareness and the need to talk are also experienced by parents and families of learners with special needs. In the UAE, the media writes more and more about 'battles' of parents to include their children in mainstream schools (7 days, Gulf news). During an interview a high official from the Ministry of Education revealed that the Ministry supports and reinforces parents who stand for the inclusion of their children. He believes that the parents' position increases the success of the included case. This resulted in the school year 2007 witnessing several cases of inclusion in government schools ("57 Special Needs Students," 2007). Some of the private schools followed suit and opened their doors to different local and expatriate children with disabilities.

Nevertheless, in the UAE, a traditionally Muslim country, some people still hold the belief that a child with special needs is a test from God and not much can be done to change his/her situation. Out of pity, some go to the length of fulfilling the merest wishes or needs of the child, and do not bother to teach the child self-help skills. In one of the richest countries of the world, with a relatively high standard of living, many families also opt for hiring a helper to take charge of the child and hence alleviate some of his/her responsibilities, away from the education of the school. Similar cases demonstrate that the "chances of inclusion, and other forms of educational services for such children, are affected by the construction of society as well as traditional values and beliefs" (Gaad, 2004, p. 315).

As far as schools are concerned, there can be a conflict of attitudes when it comes to the implementation of inclusion. Many school officials, for example, claim that their doors are open to all and that they have no objections to admitting different types of learners. When it comes to practice, however, schools worry about their academic reputation, and find excuses to reject learners with special needs. Many schools are still rigid towards making adjustments in their school buildings, curriculum, support services or teaching instructions to fit more needs. One principal of a private mainstream school in Dubai admitted a wheelchair user in one year, and let him go the following year, because the student's class moved upstairs and the school was not equipped with elevators and, in a fixed class system, rather than moving classrooms according to abilities or grades, the school was not prepared to move classrooms to the ground floor to facilitate inclusion for the concerned student. The family was devastated and complained to the educational zone, but in the end, it was just one more fight to face in the inclusion experience of the student.

In a country where the UN convention on disability that stresses inclusive education for such individuals—which was signed (March 2008) but not yet ratified—the schools generally fall under two categories: schools that claim they have no learners with special needs, and schools that declare they are ability-friendly and open to all backgrounds but may have issues on a practical level. Following the natural rates of 12–15% of the school population with educational needs, the first category of schools largely fails to provide for the needs or leaves them to the care of the parents. For the schools that accept learners with different/additional abilities, the majority charge considerable amounts of money to parents for provision of a shadow teacher and/or resources, a fact that adds to the burden of the family and makes inclusion a feared necessity rather than a chance for education.

## 3.7   DECISION-MAKING FOR EFFECTIVE INCLUSION: ISSUES AND CONCERNS

According to a top government official who was interviewed for this chapter, including learners with special needs in regular schools is just a step away from being successful. This is due to the pressure from NGOs and parents for the implementation of the first UAE law that protects the rights of people with disabilities, and that includes, naturally, those with special needs. Although by implementation of the law (known as the decree because it is a presidential federal law) schools will open up to learners with special needs, there are still many issues which need to be tackled before one can see the effect of the new legislation.

Bradshaw et al. (2004) assert that the services provided to special needs learners from the public sector focus on early intervention. A team of professionals (educational psychologists and/or speech-language pathologists) assess special needs learners as young as first grade and kindergarten. Learners with more obvious physical characteristics (such as Down syndrome) are not welcomed into the public school sector at all. According to Gaad (2004), learners with obvious exceptional intellectual learning needs are denied access to mainstream schools. In fact, parents of learners with severe disabilities, especially intellectually related ones, are usually asked to enrol their learners at special needs centres—previously known as 'preparation and rehabilitation of the handicapped'—provided by the MOSA. Regrettably, such centres usually have long waiting lists and they are designated mainly for 'national' students (Bradshaw et al., 2004). Neurological development disorders that may hinder social interaction, such as autism spectrum disorder, have few specialized centres: public and private. Unfortunately, privately-owned centres usually charge high fees (as high as AED 26,000 which was equivalent to approximately $US 7,200 in the 2007/2008 academic year). Many ethical issues can be raised here; however, sadly the high fees are not the only issue. Some parents have complained to a local newspaper that there are more than 70 learners on the waiting list for one of the special centres (Ahmad, 2006).

But what is delaying a wealthy nation like the UAE from implementing inclusion like other nations did? Is the picture in the UAE that gloomy? According to Gaad et al. (2006), ministries of education must recognize the objectives of education, and those objectives need to be highlighted within the context of the curriculum. There should be interrelationships between the society and culture from one side, and those goals from the other side. These interrelationships must be expressed either implicitly or explicitly in those goals.

## 3.8 DISCUSSION

The UAE as a society is rich in its heritage and culture. The fact that this country is diverse in a number of aspects compounds the issues it faces. The lack of uniformity within the UAE educational system does not help those with special needs or anyone who is differently able. Previous research-based studies showed that the UAE society is a caring one (Gaad, 2001). Islamic teachings affect greatly the attitudes of people in the UAE. Islam teaches its followers to take care of the 'weak.' Though the society does not abuse the 'handicapped,' as they are referred to in many parts of the region and the UAE, it does not like to mingle with 'disabled' ones (Gaad, 2001). Beside schools, the MOE's role in managing certain aspects of inclusive education and encouraging schools that initiate inclusion is crucial. The lack of sufficient data regarding learners that need to be included, and the evaluation of the experiences of the cases that have been previously included by schools are issues that need to be prioritized for effectively running inclusive practices. To insure smooth transition of services and resources, effective and well-planned collaboration between the MOE and the MOSA need to happen expediently to assess the education services offered in the various centres, and to plan to allocate human and physical resources for the UAE schools.

Whether the UAE chooses to move from the traditional segregated model of service delivery to inclusive schooling in one phase or do it through a carefully studied transition (York 1993, in Gaadc, 2004, p. 325), it is important to keep track of the progress and assess the results. Exemplary schools that attempt to include learners with various special needs and involve restructuring of their programs (Gaad, 2004, p. 325) should be supported and guided. Exceptional teachers who act upon their beliefs and exert effort and time to cater to learners with disabilities should be morally and financially praised. Forms of media that exhibit stories of people with special needs to raise awareness and act as advocates for their inclusion in the society should be saluted and encouraged. Finally, families of learners with special needs should be assisted in any way possible. Their learners are different, but have equal rights to belong and prosper.

From the 1990s onwards, inclusion has become a central concept in international policies (Arnesen, Mietola, & Lahelma, 2007) and the UAE is no exception. Inclusion, however, has issues all over the world, owing to its inherent nature, such as rigid curricular and assessment specifications, diverse learning needs, curriculum delivery etc. (Wedell, 2005). The UAE will need to tackle its own issues effectively to make room for the fundamental principles of inclusion, otherwise inclusion will be relegated to being a social problem. Taking all of the aforementioned into consideration, the application of inclusion into the educational system in UAE requires tremendous effort. In essence, there are barriers to inclusion in the UAE. These barriers may be divided into three categories: legal, ethical and cultural. However, one must be cautioned that these categories do not have to be exclusively separated. In fact, on many occasions these categories do overlap.

This is only a humble attempt to underline the running current debates and issues related to inclusive education in this relatively young but fast developing nation. No-one can claim to have a good record in tackling all related issues in regards to the adoption of effective inclusive education, and the UAE is not any different. It is argued however that understanding is the most essential step towards solving a problem. This chapter explored the main issues for a better understanding.

# 4 Inclusive Education and Cultural Challenges in the Arabian Gulf and the Middle East

Culture is unique to a particular group of people that share all aspects of life in common (Cardwell, Clark, & Meldrum, 2004, p. 953) and can be further defined as including all aspects "relating to the ideas, customs and social behaviour of a society" (Soanes & Stevenson, 2003, p. 422). One can argue that the region concerned in this book is made up of a complex mix of different cultures, each viewing individuals with disabilities from their own traditions and different beliefs, resulting in the holistic needs of such individuals being met in varied ways and levels of effectiveness accordingly. Nevertheless, the region, due to many factors including geographical and in some cases religious bonds, shares a rather 'common' cultural understanding of special needs and disabilities that affects the way policies are produced and provisions are made. This common understanding is largely much based on supporting the 'weak and vulnerable' from a charity-based approach rather than supporting citizens with equal rights and benefits from a rights-based approach as the region is still in a transitional phase between the two notions.

## 4.1 INCLUSIVE EDUCATION AND CULTURAL BELIEFS ABOUT DISABILITIES

Though most of the countries that are examined in this book have a number of legislations that have been turned out quite regularly with regard to the child with disabilities especially over the last decade, what ails any given country's progress is the variety of legal, social, economic, educational, and ethical issues that contribute to the formation of a set of cultural beliefs about disabilities as a topic, or an issue or about individuals with disabilities as a group of individuals within such a culture. Such cultures of the Gulf States, for example, have an understanding about disabilities and individuals with disabilities, that in some respects is common to the world in general, but more often than not is specific to such countries as a region. The fact that such countries may be diverse in a number of aspects compounds the issues they face.

This chapter endeavors to look at the cultural issues that stand in the way of the region providing the benefits of inclusion to its children with special needs and disabilities. Considering the fact that such 'cultural' issues are complicated, for the purposes of clarity, it is safe to state that there is a lot of overlap between the issues mentioned within each of these areas; however, a broad framework such as the that just outlined will help us examine the main players or influences in the move towards inclusion.

The concept of inclusive education has been gaining momentum around the world, by virtue of it being included in policies of international organizations such as the United Nations. Equality and human rights are the main cornerstones of documents seeking inclusion for children with special needs and disabilities. Care and concern for individuals having special needs and/ or disabilities has been a component of both heritage and culture from time immemorial. Challenge lies, however, in identifying and meeting the needs of individuals and how cultural understanding, or perhaps misunderstanding, of their needs can play a role in such a caring process. Gaad (2004c) stated that attitudes towards inclusion are affected by cultural beliefs and values. The Middle East is no different, and the entire region, as a whole, has been working towards inclusion of its disadvantaged children. However, one might find it difficult to discuss inclusion of such learners in the Gulf and the Middle East without examining cultural beliefs and attitudes related to disability in this dynamic, and, to a certain extent, restless, yet traditional region, where cultural beliefs can play a vital role in forming people's attitudes towards other individuals and groups within society. Therefore, it is safe to say that although educational systems in the region may vary, cultural attitudes towards individuals with special needs and disabilities are definitely a common factor that plays a role in shaping some elements of such systems.

Despite sharing some basic tenets, working definitions of special education vary. The overall opinion is that special education is a process that aims at meeting the individualized needs of all students in a manner that helps each one reach his or her potential.

With this in mind, it can be argued that when we use a label such as 'special needs,' there is often an inherent assumption that the problem resides within the student rather than the surroundings. Accepting such a hypothesis affects not only the way we assess but also the way we perceive, and provide flexibility in programming for such individuals.

If one tried to look at a definition of 'inclusion' from an international perspective, we may find that 'inclusion' has proved a difficult word to define. One of the favourite definitions used by human rights advocates is "[a] broad concept dealing with educational access, support for learning and equal opportunities for all pupils, whatever their age, gender, ethnicity, attainment and background." (OFSTED, 2000, cited in Jones & Smith. 2004, p. 115).

Whereas educationalists may tend to go for other definitions, Meijer at al. (1997, cited by Bradley in Hayden & Thompson, 2000) explain that "it means that students with special needs are entitled to have their special needs met in regular education . . . it stands for an educational system that encompasses a wide diversity of students and that differentiates education in response to this diversity." The CSIE[1] list the principles of the philosophy as:

- All children have the right to learn and play together.
- Children should not have to be devalued or discriminated against by being excluded or sent away because of their disability or learning difficulty.
- There are no legitimate reasons to separate children for the duration of their schooling. They belong together rather than need to be protected from one another (cited in Tilstone, Florian, & Rose, 1998, p. 14).

Tilstone et al. (1998) believe that the only definition, which transcends the concept of normalisation,[2] is given by Inclusion International (1996): Inclusion refers to the opportunity for persons with a disability to participate fully in all of the educational, employment, consumer, recreational, community and domestic activities that typify every day society (cited by Florian in Tilstone et al., 1998, p. 16).

From an international perspective, Arnesen, Mietola, and Lahlma (2007) draw on Befring's (2002) definition, which, in accordance with international policy, defines inclusion in terms of "democratic values and ideals, which" are "closely linked to the whole life and societal perspectives, as well as experiences of belonging and acceptance" (p. 000).

From the 1990s onwards inclusion has become a central concept in international policies (Arnesen et al., 2007), gradually replacing the *integration* of the 1970s, which focussed more on the location-related placement of children with SEN into mainstream settings, rather than the quality of that experience. 'Inclusion' in contrast to integration is a move to overcome "a history of exclusion" that "requires fundamental changes in thinking about the patterns of life and conditions of everyday living" (Florian, in Tilstone et al., 1998, p. 15). The task for inclusion, Florian argues, "is to redefine these things so that people with disabilities are valued for who they are because of rather than despite difference" (in Tilstone et al., 1998, p. 15).

Those who advocate inclusion argue that it is ethically wrong to deny some children an equal right to education. This stance is reflected in recent international conferences such as that held by UNESCO in Salamanca, Spain (1994). The resulting statement on "Principles, Policy and Practices in Special Needs Education and a Framework for Action" (UNESCO, 1994) notes that "every child has a fundamental right to education" and that "those with special educational needs must have access to regular schools which should accommodate them within a child-centred pedagogy capable of meeting those needs." It further calls on all governments to "give the highest policy and budgetary priority to improve their education systems to enable them to include all children regardless of individual differences or difficulties" and to adopt, "as a matter of law or policy the principle of inclusive education, enrolling all children in regular schools, unless there are compelling reasons to do otherwise." The inclusion of children with disabilities is now also an essential part of the UN's 'Education for All' programme (Bradley, in Hayden & Thompson, 2000, p. 32).

The "new dawn" Bradley describes where people are demanding a "curriculum for the 21st century that goes far beyond traditional academic domains" (Udvari-Solner & Thousand, 1995, cited in Bradley, 2000, p. 000) seems to be fast rising in the international context. "Families throughout the world," Bradley argues, citing Mittler (1995), "are striving for, and insisting upon, community-based education and many schools are opening their doors" (p. 000). This "multinational commitment," as Clough (1998) terms it, has "significant implications for those who teach in international schools," Bradley claims. The question, she warns, is not "'Is inclusion the right thing to do?', but rather 'How can inclusion best be implemented?'" (p. 33).

Unfortunately, the history of many cultures often reveals negative cultural attitudes towards individuals with special needs and disability. Since the discovery of crude oil and the strategic investment of the financial resources this provided, much of the Gulf region has developed rapidly over the last 40 years and has "emerged into the mainstream of modernism" over that short space of time. As it has grown commercially it has also diversified culturally (Gaad, 2006).

Besides the complexity of what is 'cultural' in a multi cultural region, not a great deal is recorded or mentioned about how such individuals were treated and culturally constructed in the Gulf and the Middle East apart from Egypt. In ancient Egypt, along with other nations like Sparta at the time, there are clear historical evidences of cruelty towards such individuals. A state council of inspectors examined neonates. If they suspected that a child was 'defective' in any way, the infant was thrown from a cliff to its death. By the second century AD, individuals with disabilities, especially intellectual disabilities, including children who lived throughout the Roman Empire, were frequently sold to entertain or amuse the privileged classes. Christianity led to a decline in these barbaric practices and a movement towards care for the less fortunate; in fact, all of the early religious leaders, Jesus, Buddha, Mohammed and Confucius, advocated humane treatment for individuals with disability such as the 'mentally retarded,' 'developmentally disabled' or 'infirm' (Sheerenberger, 1983, cited in Gaad, 2004). It is from here that modernist beliefs and practices of charity date.

Arabs, however, always had their own preserved 'cultural' set of beliefs about the weak and vulnerable members of their 'proud' society. Humans think in stereotypic way. For people with disability, these are usually negative. We discriminate against people we perceive as different (Ralph, 2007), adding: "If you see only the disability that will influence the way you think about disabled people and reflect your behaviour towards them, what you write and how you film issues related to disability and disabled people." Many argue that a child with disability in an Arabic country maybe more expected to be stereotyped and be a 'natural candidate' for exclusion (Gaad, 2001); whereas Mallett, (2009) argues that "the use of 'stereotypes' as a mechanism to reveal representations of disability as negative and disabling provides the capacity to support claims of discrimination towards disabled people" (p. 4).

Some interesting facts emerged when examining current cultural attitudes towards people with disabilities in the Middle Eastern countries concerned. If one looks, for example, at Tunisia and Egypt, despite the fact that they are both geographically located in Africa, typical African beliefs and attitudes towards people with disabilities are absent. African culture mostly still often views disability negatively and as something to be feared and avoided based on the belief that the "disability is the result of sorcery and witchcraft" (Francis & Muthukrishna, 2004, p. 113). This is often taken further where children with disabilities are labelled as being bewitched or carriers of an evil spirit[3] (Francis & Muthukrishna, 2004, p. 113; Abosi and Ozoji, 1985, cited in Gaad, 2004, p. 314). Francis and Muthukrishna explain further that these negative culturally-driven misconceptions are found throughout all levels of society including "parents, educators and students,", where the parents of a disabled baby are often ostracised by their immediate families. (2004c: 311).

In contemporary Egyptian society, research has shown also that the appearance of a child with an obvious disability plays a key role in placing that child in a special school on an automatic basis. Previous research showed that a child is judged by how s/he looked and by what s/he could not do rather than by what s/he could do (Gaad, 1998). Children with intellectual disabilities in Egypt have been marginalised for so long that it is considered a treat to be in a special school. Fear of failing the exams, which means in the Egyptian context the failure of the teacher, was another issue to add to the list of causes that formed such a negative attitude—that is, in addition to the lack of supportive legislation (Gaad, 2004c).

In Tunisia, the lack of published materials in English has hindered the inclusion of recent literature in the field of inclusive education. However, as rightly said by a Tunisian fellow educationalist, "Tunisia is still more French than Arabic, and despite slow change towards Arabanising the nation, it will be like this for generations to come." Such 'French,' rather rights-based attitudes towards inclusion, were apparent in the Tunisian system discussion in Chapter 2.

On the other hand, in an attempt to get views from the Gulf, I refer to Gaad (2003), who conducted a 9-month study into the first case of inclusion regarding a child with autism spectrum disorder (ASD) in the UAE. She discovered that, until recently, very little was known about ASDs in the UAE and very few specialised centres existed except for those catering to mental and severe behavioural disabilities. She describes the emergence of the Abu Dhabi Autism Centre, which was initially where 'Ali,' the subject of her study, was educated. An autism centre now also exists in Dubai. Gaad found that the process of including Ali in a local government school was partly hindered by ingrained beliefs, such as those of a top official responsible for placement in the Ministry who stated to the mother of the child: "Your son was not meant to be in a normal school my dear. God created us all with different levels of thinking and abilities. You should concentrate on his strong skills, and hobbies in the centre and develop them" (Gaad, 2003, p. 11). Gaad also stated that there are a hindering range of other missing factors she considered vital for successful inclusion in the region, namely: teacher and teacher 'helper' training; peer awareness; legal backing; parent-school collaboration; careful planning and the development of a learning community; and, a lack of societal and professional knowledge and awareness about the condition (Gaad, 2003, cited in Kite, 2008).

The impact of the media cannot be discounted as it has a large influence in the Middle East in general and in the Gulf States in particular. It plays a significant role in forming people's attitudes towards people with disabilities, and it gives the seeker an understanding of how a certain culture constructs and treats people with disabilities. In the United Kingdom—a country which is reasonably advanced in its treatment of the disabled—a recent extensive survey by Robertson (2009) of five leading UK newspapers reveals wide-ranging variation in coverage of one of the most researched disabilities: ASD. His analysis found variation from a tendency to rely on medical establishment sources in some to an apparently pro-choice, anti-establishment campaign in others but, generally, a neglect of the perspective of articulate autistics themselves. Based on an enhanced content analysis of all (179) reports on autism or Asperger's syndrome, over the 12 months of 2006, in the *Daily Telegraph* (London), *Daily Mail* (London), the *Sun* (London), the *Herald* (Glasgow), and the *Daily Record* (Glasgow), the findings were discussed using several hierarchy of influences models. However, the most important finding was that the concerns of many about the impact of 'guided' media on people's attitudes to certain disabilities were confirmed. Robertson (2009) described how it was "fairly clear in the results" that many of Shattock's concerns about press coverage of autism were true and confirmed a tendency for government supporting newspapers (*Herald, Record, Sun*) to align with mainstream professional groups and for right-wing newspapers (*Telegraph* and *Mail*) to campaign on parents' rights and to present minority academic perspectives in their support. Also, his fourth concern about inaccurate or selective reporting of scientific findings is reinforced by this analysis (Robertson, 2009, p. 26).

If one looks at Middle Eastern and Gulf media, we may not find the issue as complicated as in other countries in terms of government versus right-wing lobbies; however, we can sense the cultural attitudes towards marginalising of and, in some cases, manipulation of people with disabilities and current use of a 'charity' based rather than a 'rights' based approach when dealing with any issues to do with disabilities.

The following are some extracts of daily newspapers from the area: published on Sunday, 4 February, 2007, UAE, reporting under the title: "Ex-Cop in Murder Quiz":[4]

A former police officer has been arrested in connection with the shooting a **wheelchair-bound** lottery winner. Anderson Silva Souza, who denied involvement, turned himself in with a lawyer and is being interrogated. Souza is suspected in the shooting of Renne Senna, who won 52 million reals (dhs91.3m) in July 2005. (emphasis added)

In a famous column known as Wednesday, 21 February 2007, Letters to the Editor,[5] dated Tuesday, 7 November 2006, a portrayal of self-pity is apparent:

Shocking lack of tuition for the *handicapped*. I am an Indian working in Dubai for Danzas. I live in the Al Tawoon area and work in the Jebel Ali Port and Free Zone. . . . Travelling takes up a lot of my time as must be obvious from the two locations. I *suffered an* attack of polio when I was about two years old or so and it left me *minus the use* of both legs. I use crutches and wear a brace on my right leg which is *more afflicted* than the left one. I have been enquiring all over the place to find out which driving school in Dubai offered facilities for **someone like me** to be able to go through the lessons and appear for a test to obtain a driving license. But unfortunately, I have turned up a blank. Finally I discovered that the Sharjah Driving School next to the new Traffic Authority Building is the only one with such a service being offered. Why are the driving schools in Dubai not catering to the needs of the *handicapped*? Surely, I could not be the only one in need? (emphasis added)

Though the issue of 'rights-based' provision is often represented in the media to reflect how people with disabilities are constructed as rather vulnerable and more likely to have their rights abused, in the same popular column a complainer stated:

No-one is ever fined for using disabled Spaces. Sunday, 19th November, 2006. Why shouldn't we use handicapped parking spaces? We all know that they are just there so the shopping malls can look trendy and politically correct. First of all there are no handicapped people in Dubai. You **can't** come here If you're handicapped and you certainly **won't be given** a job by most employers. I often take advantage of these conveniently located spaces—especially in hot weather and when I'm carrying my one year old son. You'd be foolish not to. If I'm ever confronted I just **effect a slight limp**. As for fines has anyone actually seen cars being fined for parking in a **handicapped** space? (UAE, Wednesday, 21 February, 2007)[6]

In Egypt, a collection of daily newspapers and magazine articles over period of 3 months were examined to reflect current attitudes towards people with disability in and outside of educational settings. The terms used were mostly negative, such as 'suffers from,' 'afflicted with,' 'bound,' confined,' 'sentenced to,' 'prisoner of a wheelchair or wheel chair bound' and 'victim of disability.'

Historically, a commonly-held cultural belief was that children with disabilities in general, and those with intellectual disabilities in particular, resulted from some kind of an 'abnormal' sexual relationship. It is known that the ancient Greeks thought that such children would weaken their great culture, and exterminated children observed to have intellectual disabilities in a cruel and inhumane way. Clearly recognisable handicapped babies (those with Down syndrome would be a case in point) were put out on the hillside to starve or to be taken by wild animals (Stradford & Gunn, 1996, cited in Gaad, 2001).

If we attempt to look at current cultural attitudes towards individuals with special needs and disabilities in the region, we may not find as much cruelty as in the ancient days; however, there are many negative cultural attitudes that are still associated with such individuals and affect their educational and social inclusion. Social acceptance of learners with special needs and disabilities is a very important factor in any attempt to include them in schools. Sen (2000) has pointed out that peer acceptance is not something that is automatic, and very often needs to be worked on. Society, on the whole in this region, has a long way to go in terms of acceptance of disability. Inappropriate media portrayal of disabilities does not help this issue.

Pre-existing beliefs about special needs and disability play a very important role in forming the current cultural attitudes. It is safe to say that whereas some cultures in the region have acknowledged the rights of individuals with special needs and disabilities, such cultures are yet in the transitional phase from the 'charity based approach' to the 'rights based approach,' and the majority of such cultures in the region have had, and are still having, their own 'teething problems' while coming to terms with this dramatic change.

The attitude of a given community toward people with disabilities will affect the

kind of provision made for such individuals (Gaad, 2004). Schools themselves take no responsibility for the education of child, preferring instead to be looked upon as doing a favour for the child (Iyanar, 2000).

In an ideal world, and providing that laws and regulations are clearly supportive of adopting inclusive practice in the region, at the end of the day, delivery on any inclusive practice relies heavily on schools on the ground. The Middle East and the Gulf region are no different from other parts of the world despite very unique cultural practices. Ambiguity of provisions and concessions still plays a role in forming cultural attitudes as the 'old ways' of thinking that form cultural attitudes towards individuals with special needs and disabilities could be difficult to change. That could be due to a simple reason and that is the gap between 'stating' the rights-based approach in dealing with disability related issues, and actually adopting such an approach on an implementation level. As Sen (2000) argues, every board of education has its own set of concessions and provisions for the child facing a learning difficulty or disability. However, schools delivering the curriculum are very often unaware of them. As a result, children needing them are deprived of them. There is no clear, easy procedure to gain these provisions either.

A recent research based study on the inclusion of a certain category of learners with special needs in one Gulf State by Kite (2008) showed that, despite the evidence for inclusion of pupils with certain types of special needs such as ASDs at this stage of the research, there is also evidence that they are frequently refused admission. This reveals that even with the support of some legislation[7] cited by Arif and Gaad (2008), which states that "all children have the right to enter mainstream school," it is still only in the early stages of implementation with regard to most schools. Kite states that many reasons are given by schools for the rejection of such pupils, and a number of these are recognised by current research as barriers to inclusion, but most of all, is the attitude that the needs of the pupils are 'too severe' and pupils should be in special needs centres. This aligns with Gaad (2001) and Alghazo and Gaad (2004) research findings regarding the negative attitudes of officials and teachers; the belief that the pupils will not be able to access the curriculum, which is indicative of a lack of flexibility on the part of the schools (e.g. Jordan & Jones, 1999; Sicile-Kira 2003 cited in Kite 2008).

## 4.2  CONCLUSION

In light of the issues impacting the process of inclusion in this very special region, and even the outlook of society on individuals with special needs and disabilities, it is apparent that, although some Middle Eastern countries, as well as Gulf
States, are trying to 'do the right thing' by introducing inclusive practice that involves educating all children of the same peer age in the same class with suitable learning goals, it may be a longer road for them if these issues are not recognized and addressed simultaneously. The need to be seen as forward thinking countries has to be translated into action. Inclusion has issues all over the world, owing to its inherent nature, such as rigid curricular and assessment specifications, diverse learning needs, curriculum delivery etc. (Wedell, 2005). It seems also that whereas most Middle Eastern

cultures are on the quest for inclusion, they are all working in relative isolation.

More 'dialogue' is needed to highlight the issue. A policy of inclusion needs to ensure that conferences on inclusive education are open and available to all teachers and other management, as well as paraprofessionals, for collaboration to become more commonplace and for links to be forged across nations as well as schools. Breaking across cultural barriers and opening up debate and discussion about good practice will also avoid the difficulties experienced by all involved due to rights-based attitudes towards handling inclusion not quite being there yet, despite isolated and rather scattered effort to endorse such attitudes.

# 5 Discussion

This is a concluding chapter that sums up the previous chapters and critically examines the findings in light of the relevant literature. It ends with a look into the future and examination of what could be learnt from such a cross cultural examination of the concerned nations quest for inclusion.

## 5.1 ISSUES AND CHALLENGES RELATED TO INCLUSIVE EDUCATION IN THE MIDDLE EAST: DISCUSSION

Though special education in developed countries has made great strides in providing the appropriate needs for several individuals, it can be said that it is relatively new in this region. As Brock and Griffin (2000) have noted, the provision of suitable educational opportunities for people with special educational needs is a worldwide concern. How pressing this concern is in the Middle East is worth exploring.

The following are some of the issues that arose from researching inclusive education in the nine concerned countries.

### 5.1.1 Social Stigma Associated With Individuals With Special Needs and Disabilities in the Region

Historically the people of this region have not had a very open and accepting attitude towards those with special needs and/or disabilities. As Gaad (2004) noted, the type of provisions made for individuals with disabilities in any given community is affected by the attitude of that community towards these individuals. Whether the country is a cosmopolitan one that has, to a great extent, retained the cultural beliefs of its people at least amongst themselves, despite the British influence as in the case of some Gulf States, or sinking in political issues and daily wars where saving lives is the main priority every day as in Palestine, or struggling for identities where Arabic is hardly spoken and French influence still plays a huge role in societal beliefs as in the case of Tunisia, the types of provisos are hugely affected by attitudes towards such individuals.

Attitudes of teachers are the most important of all. Alghazo and Gaad (2004; citing Bacon & Schultz, 1991), Stewart (1990) and Beckwith and Matthews (1994) have noted that teachers' attitudes is a key factor that affects the relationships with students with special needs, whether they are included in a regular classroom and the quality of their lives. Alghazo and Gaad also mention that appropriate planning is necessary to effect a change in attitude. Though these awareness campaigns would be very useful, they should not be stand alone campaigns: Workshops and seminars to educate teachers and principals on the concepts and range of special educational needs would be beneficial if included. Alghazo and Gaad also argued that the severity of disability plays a significant role in accepting such children in inclusive setting.

Pre-assumptions and cultural attitudes towards certain special needs and disabilities could not be ignored. Cornwall and Robertson (1999) support the assumption that refers to the quantity of general information and skills regarding special educational needs that have to be acquired by teachers where medical conditions are present, and that hinder the acceptance of children and increase teachers' fear of including them in their classroom because of complications that may require skills that teachers simply do not have. The stigma associated with severe cases and the call for a collaborative approach to meet the complex needs of people with profound and multiple learning disabilities to facilitate their inclusion was acknowledged by Lacey and Ouvry (1998).

## 5.1.2   Issues Related to Terminology and Definition of Individuals With Special Needs

Fredrickson and Cline (2002) noted the UK legal definition of special educational needs (SEN) as follows:

> [C]hildren are said to have SEN if they require special educational provision if they have a significantly greater difficulty in learning than the majority of children of their age or because they suffer from a disability which prevents or hinders them from making use of the educational facilities provided for children of their age (Department of Education and Science 1981, Department of Education and Employment 1996). (p. 65)

It is obvious that despite an agreement on the need to provide for such individuals, the boundaries surrounding labelling and categorisation are relatively blurred in the region. This is apparent in the case of one of the most common causes of special needs worldwide—that is, learning difficulties. The concept of learning difficulties can be seen to apply specifically to any child for which these "difficulties were assessed as significantly different from those of their peers" (Beveridge, 1999, p. 1). There are huge issues in connection to diagnosis of special needs in the Middle Eastern system. Findings show that terminology used to refer to certain special needs and disabilities is often 'confusing' in the region. In the Gulf States, centres for people with special needs, formally known as Centres for the Rehabilitation of the Handicapped (Gaad, 2001), are of a rehabilitative nature, and practice under the Ministry of Social Affairs (Bradshaw, Tennant, & Lydiatt, 2004). Whereas certain provisions are designated to certain types of special needs and/or disabilities such as the resource rooms created across the Gulf States to support those with learning difficulties, they are also part of the school system, managed and regulated by the Ministry of Education. In other Middle Eastern countries, other provisions are open for all rather severe disabilities such as special schools in Egypt and Palestine that run under the authority of the country's Ministry of Education with no clear intention of changing such setting in the long term despite the interest from the public and some advocacy groups in the issue of inclusion as a means of eradicating the social stigma associated with individuals who differ in any way.

### 5.1.3 Issues Related to Policies and Legislations Related to Inclusion in the Region

No discussion related to provision for those with special needs in a given society or part of the world would be complete if inclusion and inclusive policies were not included, as they are present in almost all aspects related to education at present. Therefore, it is of importance to discuss the variation as well as the similarities in the way inclusion was explored, enforced or ignored by different countries with their respective policies.

Looking at policies from across the region, we find a great deal of similarity in the way inclusion was mentioned despite the fact that the terms and references varied from one country to another, especially in the Gulf States. The rights-based approach to inclusion as the recommended provision was stressed by many policies and legislations, however most of the articles and subsections were rather vague. A good example is in Articles 13 and 14 of the Emirati Federal Law 29/2006 on the rights of persons with disabilities which contains a statement that encourages the school to accept the child with special needs but does not, at the same time, enforce the law in a way that if a school refuses to admit a child because of his or her special needs it will be considered as breaking the law. If one looks at earlier legislations in the same subject from the same country, such as Articles 5, 6, 7 and 8 of Policy 2/385/1988 in the establishment and organisation of special classrooms in mainstream schools, one finds a change in the terminology; for example the term 'slow learner' was comfortably used, whereas almost 20 years later it was substituted with 'those with learning difficulties.' Therefore, there may be a change in the quantity of legislations, and the reference to individuals with special needs following the UN Convention on the Right of Persons With Disabilities that was adopted by the United Nations General Assembly on 13 December 2006, then opened for signature on 30 March 2007, and finally put into force on 3 May 2008.

The impact of laws and regulations on the lives of learners with special needs can be seen in Kuwait, the first country in the Gulf area to issue a designated law to regulate and protect the rights of persons with disabilities (the law was issued in 1996). The outcomes were far from inclusive: In fact, until this date, despite Article 16 of the Kuwaiti Law that established the Higher Council for Disability Affairs (HCDA), the system is based on segregating disabilities to be educated in isolation in designated schools under the Ministry of Education.

By contrast, the tiny Kingdom of Bahrain—that was voted in 2010 the most friendly country on Earth following years of Canadian domination of the title—took the issue of inclusion as a human rights issue as part of its constitution and promised in 2006 to "train Ministry of Education teachers on how to integrate the principles of human rights in all subjects" (2006 Bahrain regulation, Section 74). Reality, however, reflects teething problems in relation to implementation of such noble regulations and the commitment of the government to implement inclusion.

In larger countries like Egypt, lack of legislations altogether contributed to the delay in adopting inclusion, despite numerous advocates and non-government organisations calling for inclusion together with a number of scattered pilot projects that opened the door for selected categories of special needs to be allowed in mainstream schools.

Other international legislations, conventions and declarations have also played a role in shaping current legislations in the region with regards to rights, particularly educational rights of individuals with special needs and/or disabilities.

2006 UN Convention declarations are as follows: the United Nations Educational, Scientific and Cultural Organization  World Declaration on Education for All (UNESCO, 1990); the Salamanca Statement and Framework for Action on Special Needs Education (1994); and the Dakar Framework for Action also adopted a World Declaration on Education for All (EFA) (UNESCO, 2000).

Despite the acknowledgement of such international policies, legislations from around the region, whether or not they are enforced, are not taken seriously by those who should implement them, particularly in mainstream schools, or they are not clear enough to support inclusion and smooth transition for such learners into the mainstream world.

## 5.2   INCLUSIVE EDUCATION IN THE MIDDLE EAST: LESSONS LEARNT AND A LOOK INTO THE FUTURE

Previous chapters clearly showed that there is a kind of a 'will' to proceed with the inclusive process in most of the countries concerned, however, the 'way' is far from agreed on or achieved. Government legislation, policy, provisions and schemes illustrate that nations have good intentions and are committed to the rights of the person with disabilities. How these initiatives translate into reality is quite a different matter.

Learning from the past and starting from where others have stopped is essential if the region is to get anywhere with its inclusive policies. There is an apparent awareness issue related to individuals with special needs in the region. Looking at their disabilities rather than abilities seems to be the norm. That has a direct effect on provision and implementation even with the backup of legislation and federal laws that are, anyway, mostly ineffective because of the vagueness of some laws or of the ignorance of the public that such laws even exist in their favour. As the nine countries examined in this book are all Arab countries, the following famous Arab saying seems appropriate: "A right is never lost as long as a person demanding it exists." I do not think the region is short of people with an interest in demanding such rights, especially if laws support and grant such rights. However, in order for inclusion to be a priority on national agendas, the majority of people with a rights-based approach need to be on board. Buying-in to this approach is the way forward if an end to the struggle with implementation of inclusive policies is to be enforced.

According to Mittler (2000) cited in Kite (2008), "[I]nvesting in education, particularly that of girls, is the single most effective means of raising the standard of living and improving the health of the nation." He goes on to mention the importance of priorities in furthering this end. Within this framework of education as a basis for societal progress comes the Salamanca Statement, which came forth at a conference organized UNESCO in 1994. Salamanca reminded governments that children with disabilities and difficulties were a part of the larger group of the world's children, and that inclusion and participation of all children were essential to human dignity and the concept of human rights. It also emphasized inclusive schooling to be a major player in the achievement of these targets, and advised governments to adopt this concept as law or policy, unless they were absolutely unable to do so (Kite, 2008).

Though it is important to urge governments of the region to take immediate action to make use of laws and regulations related to inclusion of learners with special needs and/or disabilities, it is also crucial to call for something that is missing from this part of the world due to wars, political conflicts and prioritizing, and that is long-term planning for the complex inclusive policy. Kite (2008) refers to the terms 'fire fighting' and 'fire lighting' that are succinctly defined by Davidson and Pennink (2001, as cited in Kite, 2008):

> Fire fighting is what most local governments (and other organisations) are doing—focus is on current short-term problems and with limited political will or ability to think of long-term investment in managing the necessary change in the system. [Fire lighting, on the other hand is defined as] in the sense of leadership, inspirations, energy, enthusiasm,

spreading knowledge, changing culture, is what is severely lacking in many countries, but badly needed. A change in approach to capacity building from thinking about having a little more training to making a substantial long term investment in development of people and their institutions is the paradigm shift that is necessary. (p. 65)

It does not take a great deal of effort to realize that most of the region's policies and isolated efforts could easily be categorized as 'fire fighting' rather than 'fire lighting' and most of such actions exist in response to a worldwide global movement and to deflect any international criticism, rather than being part of a genuine plan for a carefully examined, long-term inclusive process.

The findings also explored the issue of voices of concerned individuals or, rather 'lack of' such voices in decision-making in the region. It is also noticed that despite some efforts in some countries to establish a higher committee for people with special needs and disabilities, the voices of such people are hardly heard.

The good old stereotypic social construction is outweighing the movement towards eradication of stigma and labelling in societies that for a long time has encouraged segregation in the name of care. It is time for the region to unite in the call for an inclusive system that takes into account individual needs as well as what those individuals and their families want. In other words, what is best for them, not just what is best for everyone else around them. This is not a call for and against inclusion as much as it is a call for allowing for more 'choices' and options for individuals with special needs and disabilities in the region's education systems.

Parents are also important stakeholders in the inclusive school, as noted by Tilstone & Florian (1998: 14). An interview with one teacher in an Emirati school in Dubai revealed the importance of collaboration: "I think for inclusion to be successful, you need that three way of parent, children and teacher working towards the goals." It is all about "sharing" responsibility (Kite, 2007).

Whether laws are effective or not, it is always a good start to have the support of legislations when it come to any human rights issue. Countries that have not issued any legislation on the rights of persons with special needs and/or disabilities should start to act as soon as possible. In the case of those countries that issued laws to protect the rights of individuals with special needs and/or disabilities, it is time to issue a 'white paper' or any form or report that makes law accessible and easy to implement. The whole notion of 'making sense of the law' and 'coming to terms with the laws' is not quite known here and might be interpreted as deviation from the law. One is not even sure if there are legal boundaries round any given expert's interpretation of the law for professional and implementation purposes. This is not only limited to this part of the world. Tilstone & Florian (1998:14) argues that

[T]here is a gap between policy and implementation which must be acknowledged and addressed. How it is that there can be so much philosophical agreement on rights and yet so much divergence in practice is not well understood. Tilstone & Floriajn (1998:14)

Describing the inclusive school is crucial to allow participants to understand in detail what makes the inclusive school differ from any other neighbourhood school. Such descriptions will help in eliminating false assumptions and myths associated with the whole process in places that have been so long used to a segregated system. Though the road to inclusion seems to be a long and winding one, it is worthwhile to keep in mind the expanse that inclusion implies.

According to Friend and Bursuck (2002, pp. 113–114, 121), the classroom environment plays a major role in student learning, with key areas being classroom organisation, classroom grouping, instructional materials and instructional methods.

Mittler (2000, p. 75) points out that although the characteristics of effective schools could be described as 'inclusion-friendly,' they are more neutral than proactive, as the core of inclusion involves structural and curricular reorganisation in order to meet the needs of all students. Therefore, the inclusive classroom entails more than just allowing a child with SEN in. It also means changing structure, curriculum, planning, instruction, attitudes, beliefs and methods of collaboration. It involves commitment on the part of all players, and a constant re-evaluation of what is working and what is not: In short, it is an on-oing process.

In looking at why things exist in their current form in terms of accessibility and alteration of physical environment, it is useful to remember that "the earlier system of segregated schooling, or special schools for children with special needs, was a reflection of care, not entitlement" (Alur, 2006). This attitude is not unique to the region; it can also be found in other countries. These same special schools soon came to be thought of as the only answer for the child with SEN and hence, according to Deepa (2006), schools and colleges were built without providing any access for persons with disabilities.

Bradshaw et al. (2004) mentioned the 'anxieties' associated with the subject of special education and inclusive provision in one of the GCC countries whereas Gaad et al. (2006) suggested that curriculum development is one of the keys to a successful change towards inclusion.

Long-term curriculum planning for 'investing' in children and the so-called 'child-centred system' has not quite been considered by the concerned countries. Howard Gardner introduced at least seven intelligences in his book *Frames of Mind*. He proposed the following intelligences: logical/mathematical intelligence, verbal/linguistic intelligence, visual/spatial intelligence, bodily/kinesthetic intelligence, musical/rhythmic intelligence, interpersonal intelligence, intrapersonal intelligence (Gardner, 1983/2003) and an eighth intelligence which was added later called naturalistic intelligence. There are strong views in support of and in opposition to such a theory; however, this book is not the relevant forum for this sort of discussion. One fact worth mentioning though is that none of the discussed countries have taken into consideration multiple intelligences when providing for learners with and without special needs and disabilities.

In addition, families of learners with special needs and/or disabilities feel overwhelmed by the number of 'decisions' they have to make in life on behalf of their children, and the fact that they do not really have multiple 'choices' given the social stigma associated with the limited abilities of their children. They also have to make the 'right decisions for the future careers of their children. One can argue, however, that whether the seeker of advice on career guidance is with or without disabilities, career guidance is the most overlooked element in the education system in the Arab world (Bin Talal, 2004).

Brooks and Brooks (1999) refuse the traditional method which is based on students' receptiveness. Instead, they call for an alternative way: constructivism. They argue that in a modern system, educators should identify three ways in which students can learn: by generating, demonstrating and exhibiting. This fits perfectly into any inclusive environment. However, in most of the countries discussed in this book any inclusive attempt is bound to struggle due partly to rigid, 'one size fits all' curriculum and 'fixed' expectations of student learning and participation.

Maroun, Samman, Moujaes, and Abouchakra (2008) argued that "Arab countries, have come to identify a good education system as a cornerstone of economic progress." They added, "Recent years have witnessed many Arab countries making efforts to develop and implement comprehensive education reform programs that can result in a skilled, knowledge-based workforce in line with socioeconomic goals." The authors propose a strategy for improving the education sector, based on three elements: "defining socioeconomic priorities, developing the appropriate operating model for the sector based on those priorities, and building the educational infrastructure to support that model" (p. 1). This book argues clearly that such urgency to develop the subsystems of special needs education in the region with an inclusive agenda does not apply simply because of the fact that inclusion has not been defined as one of the socioeconomic priorities in most of the concerned countries. It is clear that despite a wide interest in the 'issue' of inclusion, actual shift of traditional systems from the care and charity-based approach to the rights-based approach is seriously lacking and not acknowledged as one of the priorities.

The nature of special education has seen a favourable change over the past few decades. According to Hoover and Patton (2008), as a result of this change, the role of a special educator needs to be examined and further developed to provide the most effective education for all learners at-risk and those with high and low incidence disabilities. Lieberman (1990) cited in

Gaad (1998) argued that if people do not see the need for change, the task of bringing about change becomes more difficult, if not impossible. The old ways will not be transformed easily unless the old ways are inadequate for the majority of people (Lieberman, 1990, cited in Gaad, 1998).

In conclusion, inclusion is not always understood or welcomed by cultures that have had segregated systems for as long as they have existed. Undoubtedly, however, there are certain activities in the area of inclusion in the region that are supported whether by federal laws or advocacy pressure towards adoption of inclusion of learners with special needs and/or disabilities in mainstream schools. By and large, despite the clear and present 'call' for inclusion that is paving the way in this unique, hospitable, albeit troubled Middle Eastern region, the serious developments that are usually associated with comprehensive policies and procedures are yet to occur.

Those who advocate inclusion sing praises of its benefits for all, including a sense of belonging to a diverse human family within which a stimulating environment to grow and learn is provided. Further to this is the enhancement of self-respect for all and affirmations of individuality plus opportunities to be educated with same-age peers.[1] The worldwide movement towards a society that is not divided due to differences in color, race, gender, class or education is a dignified cause. However, the journey towards such a society or world may well be long and may be painful, especially if it is perceived or portrayed as 'ideal' as it will have the inevitable effect of making it seem impossible to reach. Adopting the 'rights- based approach' in advocacy and in policy development will make such a world reachable and will encourage advocates and families of such individuals to call for their 'rights' rather than dreaming of a fantasy land. The role of pressure groups and governments' constant review of policies that support the rights of such people and the welfare of the child with special needs and/or disabilities is crucial. After all, children, regardless of their strengths and weaknesses, are the bearers of the future. A nation investing in its future signifies a belief in the worldwide movement towards tolerance and valuing of differences, and there is possibly not a more apt global theme for such a movement than 'children that learn together learn to live together.'[2]

# Author Biography

Dr. Eman Gaad is a Senior Lecturer at British University in Dubai's Faculty of Education, and leads the University's Masters and EdD program in Special Education with an honorary lectureship status at the reputed University of Birmingham, UK. She is also the co-founder and Executive Director of the UAE Down Syndrome Association. She was seconded as the Director of Disability Services at Dubai Government's Community Development Authority since January 2009. Dr. Gaad is internationally known as an advocate for inclusion for learners with special needs in mainstream schools and is a well published researcher and scholar in the field.

# Notes

## NOTES TO CHAPTER 1

1. Warnock, H. M., (1978a). Special Educational Needs: report of the Committee of enquiry into the Education of Handicapped Children and Young people. (Online): http://www.sen.ttrb.ac.uk/attachments/21739b8e-5245-4709-b433-c14b08365634.pdf [10/11/08]
2. CIA World fact Book link · www.theodora.com/wfbcurrent/egypt/egypt_people.html
3. https://www.cia.gov/library/publications/the-world-factbook/geos/ts.html (July 2009 est.)
4. Different geographic definitions of Palestine have been used over the millennia, and these definitions themselves are politically contentious. In recent times, the *broadest* definition of Palestine has been that adopted by the British Mandate, and that is called the Palestinian territories, which are the West Bank and Gaza Strip. Survey of Palestine, prepared in December 1945 for the information of the Anglo-American Committee of Inquiry, p. 103) stated that the area of Palestine back then was 27,024 square Kms.
5. Currently map of Palestine include Gaza Strip and that is 360 square kms and the West bank with an area of 5,957 Kms source http://www.angelfire.com/la2/lux/pgraphy.html June 2008
6. http://english.wafa.ps/?action=detail&id=12806
7. http://knowledge.moe.gov.eg/Arabic/Teacher/private/history/ June 2009
8. Republic of Tunisia, The national Reposrt 2004-2008, Ministry of Education and Training p. 4.
9. http://www.moe.gov.om/portal/sitebuilder/sites/EPS/Arabic/MOE/spedu1.aspx June 2009
10. http://www.moe.gov.om/portal/sitebuilder/sites/EPS/Arabic/MOE/spedu1.aspx June 2009

## NOTES TO CHAPTER 2

1. https://www.cia.gov/library/publications/the-world-factbook/geos/sa.html.
2. For further information on the Inclusion Project, please refer to http://www.moudir.com/vb/showthread.php?t=1608.
3. http://www.alriyadh.com/2008/10/24/article383012.html (accessed June 2008).
4. http://www.alriyadh.com/2008/10/24/article383012.html (accessed Nov 2008).
5. http://www.aifo.it/english/resources/online/books/cbr/SR-interview0506.htm The interview was conducted by Dr. Sunil Deepak from AIFO/Italy in

Cairo on 3 May 2006 during a regional meeting of the World Health Organisation (WHO) on implementation of UN Standard Rules in Eastern Mediterranean region (accessed February 2009).

6. Retrieved February 2009 from http://www.aifo.it/english/resources/online/books/cbr/SR-interview0506.htm. The interview was conducted by Dr Sunil Deepak from AIFO/Italy in Cairo on 3 May 2006 during a regional meeting of the World Health Organization (WHO) on implementation of UN Standard Rules in Eastern Mediterranean region.

7. http://www.dib-qatar.com/qatar/education.htm (accessed January 2009).

8. http://www.g111g.com/vb/t115592.html (accessed January 2009).

9. http://www.g111g.com/vb/t115592.html (accessed January 2009).

10. http://www.arabvolunteering.org/corner/avt5949.html (accessed November 2008).

11. http://www.moe.gov.om/portal/sitebuilder/sites/EPS/Arabic/MOE/spedu1.aspx (accessed January 2009).

12. http://www.moe.gov.om/portal/sitebuilder/sites/EPS/Arabic/MOE/spedu1.aspx (accessed January 2009).

13. http://forum.moe.gov.om/vb/showthread.php?t=28656 (accessed January 2009).

14. http://new.sis.gov.eg/En/Story.aspx?sid=2352 (accessed November 2009).

15. Support Education Training for Inclusion (SETI) Centre of CARITAS, an NGO, established in 1998.

16. http://weekly.ahram.org.eg/2007/851/li1.htm 28 June–4 July 2007 Issue No. 851 (accessed January 2009).

17. http://www.ashoka.org/node/2988 (accessed January 2009).

18. http://weekly.ahram.org.eg/2007/851/li1.htm 28 June–4 July 2007 Issue No. 851.

19. http://weekly.ahram.org.eg/2007/851/li1.htm 28 June–4 July 2007 Issue No. 851.

20. Results presented at the Arab rehabilitation International Regional Conference, Tunisia, 2007.

21. www.mohe.gov.ps/reema.html (accessed June 2008).

22. www.mohe.gov.ps/5year-plan/index.html (added June 2008).

23. Source, translated from Arabic Palestinian Independent Association for citizens' rights, 2006 Report 47.

## NOTES TO CHAPTER 3

1. Takamul is programme launched by the Dubai Educational Council. For more information, go to the website at http://www.takamul.gov.ae. Takamul was dismantled to another programme under the Dubai Government Community Development Authority.

## NOTES TO CHAPTER 4

1. Centre for Studies of Inclusive Education, http://inclusion.uwe.ac.uk/csie/un-draft-convention-alert.htm

2. 'Normalisation' means that children with SEN are automatically perceived to be defective and in order to participate must learn to adapt to the 'normal' environment.

3. The 'tokoloshe' is commonly known as a malevolent spirit in African culture and blamed for an unfortunate occurrence or used to scare children much like the 'bogey man' concept in Western cultures
4. 7 days of daily newspapers retrieved Thursday, 15 February 2007.
5. http://www.7days.ae/en/category/letters-to-the-editor/
6. Retrieved January 2008 from http://www.7days.ae/contact/.
7. Reference to UAE Federal Law No. 29/2006.

## NOTES TO CHAPTER 5

1. Newfoundland and Labrador Association for Community Living. Retrieved November 2009 from http://www.nlacl.ca/inclusion.html
2. Author unknown.

# Bibliography

Abood, A. A. (2005). Almaserah: Descriptive study about special education's practice in the United Arab Emirates. *Abu Dhabi: Ministry of Education Publications, Department of Special Abilities.*

Ahmad, M. (2006). Parents upset by long wait for autism help. *Emirates Today*, 6 April, p. 2.

Alghazo, E., & Gaad, E. (2004). General education teachers in the United Arab Emirates and their acceptance of the inclusion of learners with disabilities. *British Journal of Special Education*, 31(2), 94–99.

Al-Harthy, A. (1999). Drug abuse in the Gulf states/Oman: An Evaluation of The Death Penalty as a Deterrent. *Unpublished PhD Thesis.* UK, University of Manchester.

Al-Harthy, A. and Al-Adawi, S. (2002). Enemy within? The silent epidemic of substance dependency in GCC countries. *SQU Journal for Scientific Research: Medical Sciences*, Vol. 4, No.1–2 and 1–7, Sultan Qaboos University, Oman, Muscat.

Al-Nakyb, K. (2001). *Reality and the future of the social gulf situation.* Union Arabic Research Centre, Lebanon.

Al Roumi, M. (2006). *UAE keen to support special needs people.* Posted on 26 September 2006. Cited in UAE Interact on 26 December 2006. http://uaeinteract.com/default.asp (accessed December 2007).

Alur, M. (2006). Inclusive education needs funds. The Times of India [Online]. Available at http://timesofindia.indiatimes.com/articleshow/1429497.cms [2007, January 8].

Arif, M., & Gaad, E. (2008). Special needs education in the UAE: A systems perspective. *Journal for Research in Special Education*, 8(2) 111–117.

Arnesen, A. L., Mietola, R., & Lahelma, E. (2007). Language of inclusion and diversity: policy discourses and social practices in Finnish and Norwegian schools. *International Journal of Inclusive Education*, 11(1), 97–110.

Authority of Palestinian Territory1975, The special announcement on the rights of people with mental disability in Palestine.

Bacon, E. H., & Schultz, J. B. (1991). A survey of mainstreaming practices. *Teacher Education and Special Education*, 14(2), 144–149.

Bahrain Brief, (2001). *Education Reform in Bahrain*, Produced by the Gulf Centre for Strategic Studies, 2 (11). http://www.bahrainbrief.com.bh/english/nov2001-issue.htm (accessed 17/10/2007).

Barnard, J., Broach, S., Potter, D., & Prior, A. (2002). Autism in schools: Crisis or challenge. London: National Autistic Society.

Barnett, J. J., & Fallon, G. (2007). Conflicting views of school community: The dichotomy between administrators and teachers. *International Journal of Education Policy and Leadership*, 2(1), 1–11.

Beckwith, J. B., & Matthews, J. M. (1994). Measuring comfort in interacting with people with intellectual disabilities. *Australian Journal of Psychology*, 46, 53–57.

Benn, T., Pfister, G., & Jawad, H. (2010 in press) *Muslim Women in Sport and Physical Education*. London: Routledge International Series.

Beveridge, S. (1999). Special educational needs in schools (2nd ed.). London: Routledge.

Bin Talal, H. (2004). The Arab Human Development Report 2002: Review and reform. *Arab Studies Quarterly* (ASQ), 6(2).

Birkett, V. (2003). *How to support and teach children with special educational needs*. Cambridge, MA: Learning Disabilities Association of America.

Boling, E. (2007). Yeah, but I still don't want to deal with it: Changes in a teacher candidate's resistance toward inclusion. *Teaching Education*, 18(3), 217–231.

Bradshaw, K., Tennant, L., & Lydiatt, S. (2004). Special education in the United Arab Emirates: Anxieties, attitudes and aspirations. *International Journal of Special Education*, 19(1), 49–55.

Brock, C., & Griffin, R. (Eds.). (2000). Introduction. In *International perspectives on special educational needs*. Suffolk, England: John Catt Educational Limited.

Brooks, J., & Brooks, M. (1999). In search of understanding: The case for constructivist classrooms (2nd rev. ed.). Prentice Hall: Virginia. 231.

Brusling, C., & Pepin, B. (2003). Inclusion in schools: Who is in need of what? *European Educational Research Journal*, 2(2) 197–202.

Cardwell, M., Clark, L., & Meldrum, C. (2004). *Psychology*. London: Collins.

CIA—The World Factbook 2007, United Arab Emirates, viewed 8 August 2007, https://www.cia.gov/library/publications/the-world-factbook/geos/ae.html.

Clark, C., Dyson, A., Millward, A. J., & Skidmore, D. (1997). *New directions in special needs: Innovations in mainstream schools*. London: Cassell.

Clough, P. (1998). *Managing inclusive education: From policy to experience*. London: Paul Chapman.

Colebatch, J., (2002). *Policy*, second edition, Maidenhead, Open University Press.

Cornwall, J., & Robertson, C. (1999). *Physical disabilities and medical conditions: Individual education plans*. London: David Fulton.

Davidson, F., &Pennink, C. (2001). From Fire-Fighting to Fire-Lighting: International experience in capacity building and its relevance for Ethiopia. *National Seminar on Urban/Municipal Capacity Building* Addis Ababa Ethiopia 3–5 July Institute for Housing and Urban development Studies Rotterdam, The Netherlands (p 65) cited in Kite 2008 Kite, R. (2008). 'Fire fighting' or 'Fire lighting': A Critical Evaluation of the Inclusion of Children with Autism Spectrum Disorders attending Mainstream International Primary Schools in Dubai unpublished MEd dissertation, British University in Dubai.

Deepa, A. (2006). Included by law, but little else. India Together [Online]. Retrieved 2 January 2007 from http://www.indiatogether.org/2006/jan/edu-speced.htm

Dyson, A., Gallannaugh, F., & Millward, A.) 2003). Making space in the standard agenda: developing inclusive practices in schools. *European Educational Research Journal*, 2(2) pp. 228–244.

Eapen, V., Mabrouk, A., Zoubeidi, T., & Yunis, F. (2007). Prevalence of pervasive developmental disorders in preschool children in the UAE. *Journal of Tropical Pediatrics*, 53(3) 202–205.

Everard, K.B., Morris, G. and Wilson, I. (2004). Effective school management (4th Edition) London: Paul Chapman Publishing.

Farouk, K. (2008). Current status of educating Emirati learners with autism spectrum disorder in Dubai. *Unpublished MEd dissertation, British University, Dubai, UAE*.

57 special needs students join school. (2007). Khaleej Times. 7. Retrieved 30 November 2007 from http://khaleejtimes.com/DisplayArticleNew.asp?xfile=data/theuae/2007/October

Flavell, L. (2001). *Preparing to include special children in mainstream schools: A practical guide.* London: David Fulton.

Francis, D., & Muthukrishna, N. (2004). Able voices on inclusion/exclusion—people in their own words. *International Journal of Special Education,* 19(1), 107–117

Frederickson, N., & Cline, T. (2002). *Special educational needs, inclusion and diversity: A textbook.* Maidenhead, England: Open University Press.

Friend, M., & Bursuck, W. D. (2002). *Including students with special needs: A practical guide for classroom teachers.* (3rd Ed.) Boston: Allyn & Bacon.

Gaad, E. (1998). Alison and Rasha, *The experience of education of a child with Down's Syndrome in England and Egypt.* Unpublished PhD thesis, University of East Anglia, Norwich, England.

Gaad, E. (2001). Educating learners with Down syndrome in the United Arab Emirates. *British Journal of Special Education,* 28(4), 195–203.

Gaad, E. (2003, March 25–27). Ali in the regular school: The experience of educating a child with autism in the regular school in the United Arab Emirates. The Social Brain Conference, Göteborg, Sweden, 1–18.

Gaad, E. (2004a). Including learners with exceptional learning needs in regular schools in the United Arab Emirates. International Journal of Diversity in Organisations, Communities and Nations, 4, 159–165.

Gaad, E. (2004b). Pre-service teachers' attitudes towards a career in special education in the United Arab Emirates. *College Student Journal,* 38(4), 619–631.

Gaad, E. (2004c). Cross-cultural perspectives on the effect of cultural attitudes towards inclusion for learners with intellectual disabilities. *International Journal of Inclusive Education,* 8, (3), p. 311–328.

Gaad, E. (2006). The social and educational impacts of the first national Down Syndrome support group in the UAE. *Journal of Research in Special Educational Needs,* 6(3), 134–142.

Gaad, E. *A Case Study on United Arab Emirates: Women, Disability and Sport.* In Benn, T., Pfister, G. and Jawad, H. (In Press) Muslim Women in Sport and Physical Education, London: Routledge International Series.

Gaad, E., & Khan, L. (2007). Primary mainstream teachers' attitudes towards inclusion of learners with special educational needs in the private sector: A perspective from Dubai. *International Journal of Special Education,* 22(2), 95–109.

Gaad, E., & Thebet, R. (2009). Needs assessment for effective inclusion in United Arab Emirates government schools. *International Journal of Interdisciplinary Social Science,* Volume 4, Number 6, pp. 159–173.

Gardner, H. (2003). Frames of mind: The theory of multiple intelligences. New York: Basic Books. (Original work published 1983).

Hanne Eggen, R. (2007). Living with Contradiction: Examining the Worldview of the Jewish Settlers in Hebron. *International Journal of Conflict and Violence,* 1(2), 169–184

Hayden, M., & Thompson, J. (Eds.). (2000). International schools and international education: Improving teaching, management and quality. London: Kogan Page.

Hoover, J., & Patton, J. (2008). The role of special educators in a multitiered instructional system. *Intervention in School and Clinic,* 43(4) 244–251.

Ibrahim, T. (2008). Meeting the needs of mathematically adolescent gifted learners in mixed-Abilities classrooms in the private education sector of UAE: A case study. Unpublished MEd dissertation, British University, Dubai, UAE.

Iyanar, C. K. J. (2000, July 24–28). Listening to different voices—how do people with disabilities experience inclusion and exclusion in education. Paper presented at Including the Excluded, International Special Education Congress 2000,

University of Manchester, Manchester, England [Online]. Retrieved 11 January 2007 from http://www.isec2000.org.uk/abstracts/papers_i/iyanar_1.htm

Jones, J., & Smith, C. (2004). Reducing exclusions whilst developing effective intervention and inclusion for pupils with behaviour difficulties. *Emotional and Behavioural Difficulties*, 9(2), 115–129.

Jordan, R., & Jones, G. (1999). Meeting the needs of children with autistic spectrum disorders. London: David Fulton.

Khaleej Times newspaper (7 October 2007). 57 Special needs students join school. Accessed: 30 November 2007. Available at: http://khaleejtimes.com/DisplayArticleNew.asp?xfile=data/theuae/2007/October.

Kingdom of Bahrain, the 2006 Bahrain regulation, section 74.

Kite, R. (2007). Inclusion: Policy into practice. Unpublished research work. Dubai: The British University.

Kite, R. (2008), Fire Fighting or Fire Lighting? A Critical Evaluation of the Inclusion of Children with Autism Spectrum Disorders attending Mainstream International Primary Schools in Dubai. A dissertation submitted to The British University in Dubai in part fulfilment of the requirements for the degree of Masters in Education.

Kuwaiti Law 49 for the year 1996 for Disabled Matters, State of Kuwait, Ministry of Social Affairs.

Lababidi, L. (2002). *Silent no more: Special needs people in Egypt*. Cairo: American University in Cairo Press.

Lacey, P., & Ouvry, C. (1998). People with profound and multiple learning disabilities: A collaborative approach to meeting complex needs. London: David Fulton.

Lomofsky, L., & Lazarus, S. (2001). South Africa: First steps in the development of an inclusive education system. *Cambridge Journal of Education*, 31(3), 303–317.

Mallett, R. (2009). Choosing "stereotypes": Debating the efficacy of (British) disability—criticism, *Journal of Research in Special Educational Needs*, 9(1), 4–11.

Maroun, N., Samman, H., Moujaes, C., & Abouchakra, R. (2008). How to succeed at education reform: The case for Saudi Arabia and the broader GCC region. Retrieved December 2009 from http://www.booz.com/global/home/what_we_think/reports_and_white_papers/ic-display/41901870 accessed December 2009, Booz & Company Inc.

McGregor, E., & Campbell, E. (2001). The attitudes of teachers in Scotland to the integration of children with autism into mainstream schools. *Autism*, 5(2) 189–207.

Ministry of Education, KSA. (2005). The Executive Summary of The Ministry of Education Ten-Year Plan (1425–1435 H/2004–2014), Second Edition, Ministry of Education, KSA.

Ministry of Education Publications. National Report on Development of Education in Arab Republic of Egypt (2000–2004). Cairo: Author.

Ministry of Social Affairs. (2006). UAE Federal Law No. 29 of the Year 2006 on the Rights of People With Special Needs, Abu Dhabi.

Ministry of Social Development, Bahrain. (2006). Bahrain Report on Special Needs. Bahrain: Ministry of Social Affairs.

Ministry of Social Development, *Bahrain, Bahrain Report on Special Needs* 2006, published by Ministry of Social affairs, Bahrain.

Mittler, P. (2000). *Working towards inclusive education*. London: David Fulton.

National Centre for education Research and Development (2000-2004) US Department of Education.

National Report on Development of Education in Arab Republic of Egypt (2000-2004). Egypt Ministry of Education Publications.

1994 law of disabled rights in Palestine.

Palestinian Child Act. (2004).

Palestinian Government. (1994). Law of disabled rights in Palestine.

Palestinian Independent Association for Citizens' Rights. (2006). Report 47. Internest sources: www.mohe.gov.ps (accessed June 2008).

Palestinian unified regulation in 1993 on achieving equal chances for people with disabilities.

Robertson, J. W. (2009). Informing the public? UK newspaper reporting of autism and Asperger's syndrome. *Journal of Research in Special Educational Needs,* 9(1), 12–26.

Røislien, H. E. (2007). Living with contradiction: Examining the worldview of the Jewish settlers in Hebron. *International Journal of Conflict and Violence,* 1(2), 169–184.

Rugh, W. A. (1997). The United Arab Emirates: What are the sources of its stability? *Middle East Policy,* 5(3), 17.

Samail- Oman, Oman Newspaper, 16/09/2005.

Schweitzer, Yoram. (2001). Suicide bombings—the ultimate weapon? http://www.ict.org.il/index.php?sid=119&lang=en&act=page&id=5355&str=schweitzer,%20yoram (accessed August 20, 2007).

Sen, R. (2000, July 24–28). Facilitating inclusive education: The changing role of special educational centres. Paper presented at Including the Excluded, International Special Education Congress 2000, University of Manchester, Manchester, England [Online]. Retrieved 11 January 2007 from http://www.isec2000.org.uk/abstracts/papers_s/sen_1.htm

Shattock, P. (2006). The influence of the media on the MMR debate. Autism 2006 Conference, AWARES.org Conference Centre [Online]. Retrieved 24 November 2006 from http://www.awares.org/conferences/show_paper.asp?section=00010 0010001&conferenceCode=000200020034&id=107&full_paper=1

Shaw, K., Badri, A. and Hukul, A. (1995) Management concerns in the United Arab Emirates state schools. International Journal of Educational Management, 9(4), 8-13.

Sheerenberger, R. C. (1983). A history of mental retardation. Baltimore: Brookes.

Shenouda, E., & Al-Agha, S. (2009). Can special needs education institutions contribute to inclusion? The Debate. *The Disability Monitor Initiative—Middle East Journal,* 2, 34–39.

Sicile-Kira, C. (2003). *Autism spectrum disorders: The complete guide.* London: Vermilion.

Soanes, C., & Stevenson, A. (Eds.). (2003). Oxford dictionary of English (2nd ed.). Oxford, England: Oxford University Press.

Spencer, T. (2009). *An investigation into the effectiveness of the learning support room in an Emirati primary school.* Unpublished MEd thesis, British University, Dubai.

Stewart, C. (1990). Effect of practical types in preservice adapted physical education curriculum on attitudes toward disabled populations. *Journal of Teaching in Physical Education,* 10, 76–83.

Takamul, http://www.takamul.gov.ae/en/news/display.asp?id=297&hi=6

Talhami, G. H., (2004). Women, education and development in the Arab Gulf countries. Abu Dhabi: The Emirates centre for strategic studies and research.

Thomson, G., Ward, K. and Wishart, J. (1995) The transition to adulthood for children with Down's syndrome, Disability and Society, 10(3): 325–340.

Tilstone, C., Florian, L., & Rose, R. (Eds.). (1998). Promoting inclusive practice. London: Routledge.

UAE Interact (2007). *Dubai population makes big surge, posted on 01/03/2007* [online] available from http://www.uaeinteract.com/docs/Dubai_population_makes_big_surge/24196.htm [10 July 2008]

UN Convention on the Rights of Persons With Disabilities. Available at http://www.un.org/disabilities/

UNESCO. (1990). *World declaration on education for all*. Available at http://www.unesco.org/education/efa/ed_for_all/background/

UNESCO. (1994). The Salamanca statement and framework for action on special needs education. *World Conference on Special Education*, Salamanca, Spain.

UNESCO, (2000). The Dakar framework for action adopted a world declaration on education for all (EFA). Paris: Author.

Vash, C. L. (2001). Disability attitudes for all latitudes. *Journal of Rehabilitation*, 67(1), 38–42.

Vygotsky, L. S. (1978). Mind in society: The development of higher psychological processes (M. Cole, Ed.). Cambridge, MA: Harvard University Press.

Warnock, H. M., (1978a). *Special Educational Needs: report of the Committee of enquiry into the Education of Handicapped Children and Young people*. (Online): http://www.sen.ttrb.ac.uk/attachments/21739b8e-5245-4709-b433-c14b08365634.pdf [10/11/08]

Wedell, K. (2005). Dilemmas in the quest for inclusion. *British Journal of Special Education*, 32(1), 3–11.

World Declaration on Education For All. Accessed 12/13/07. Available at: http://www.unesco.org/education/efa/ed_for_all

York, J., et. al. (1993). Creating inclusive school communities. Minneapolis: University of Minnesota Press.

## WEBSITES

Al-Ahram Weekly newspaper, Egypt (2007): http://weekly.ahram.org.eg/2007/851/li1.htm 28 June–4 July 2007 Issue No. 851.

Education reform in Bahrain. (2001). Produced by the Gulf Centre for Strategic Studies, 2(11). http://www.bahrainbrief.com.bh/english/nov2001-issue.htm (accessed 17/10/2007).

USA Today - Jun 4, 2006 Educational Reforms in Saudi Arabia: We're Trying Hard to Change Prince Turki al-Faisal. http://www.saudi-us-relations.org/articles/2006/ioi/060608-saudi-textbooks.html (accessed November 2008).

Takamul. http://www.takamul.gov.ae/en/news/display.asp?id=297&hi=6

World Declaration on Education for All. http://www.unesco.org/education/efa/ed_for_all (accessed 13 December 2007).

http://www.ashoka.org/node/2988

http://inclusion.uwe.ac.uk/csie/un-draft-convention-alert.htm

https://www.cia.gov/library/publications/the-world-factbook/geos/sa.html

http://www.mohe.gov.ps/reema.html

http://www.sec.gov.qa/content/resources/detail/2286 June 2009

## OTHER SOURCES

Ralph, Dr. Sue, visiting professor, University of Northampton. (2007). Valuing difference in order to fully include disabled people in society. Presentation.

# Index

Note: Page numbers in *italics* are for tables.